Walk

בראשית

In the beginning

ויחי
וינש אליו
מקץ שנתים
וישב יעקב בארץ
וישׁלח יעקב מלאכים
ויצא יעקב מבאר שבע
תולדת יצחק בן אברהם
חיי שרה מאה שנה ואשרים שנה
וירא אליו יהוה באלני ממרא והוא ישׁב
לך לך מארצך וממולדתך ומבית אביך
נח איש צדיק תמים היה בדרתיו את האלהים התהלך
בראשית ברא אלהים את השמים ואת הארץ

Jeffrey Enoch Feinberg, Ph.D.
illustrations by Kim Alan Moudy

LEDERER

Messianic Jewish Publishers
a division of
Lederer/Messianic Jewish Communications
Baltimore, Maryland

© The Foundation for Leadership and Messianic Education, 1998. 234 Surrey Lane, Lake Forest, IL 60045

Unless otherwise noted, all Scripture quotations are taken from the *Complete Jewish Bible.* Copyright by David H. Stern, Jewish New Testament Publications, Inc., 1998.

04 03 02 01 00 99   6 5 4 3 2 1

ISBN 1-880226-75-8
Library of Congress Catalog Card Number: 99-70369

Walk GENESIS! is part of
the UMJC Special Collection
of recommended resources.

Messianic Jewish Publishers
a division of
Lederer/Messianic Jewish Communications
6204 Park Heights Avenue
Baltimore, Maryland 21215
(410) 358-6471

Distributed by
Messianic Jewish Resources International
order line: (800) 410-7367
e-mail: MessJewCom@aol.com
Internet: http://www.MessianicJewish.net

Acknowledgements

Written as a thank-you note to the Creator, *Walk GENESIS!* sings out, "Thanks, O LORD!" for providing me a library and study in the midst of a grand old forest. The manuscript would never have been completed without the tireless help of my life partner, Pat. Whatever clarity exists must be attributed to Pat's unceasing attention to shorten and simplify. Dan Swift played a key role in technical and computer support. Kim Moudy's artistic talents added another dimension for which I'm thankful.

World class scholars from Trinity International University, Dr. Richard Averbeck and Dr. Dennis Magary, read through the manuscript with an eye to keeping the work intellectually honest. Dr. John Fischer and Stuart Dauermann gave informed feedback in the earliest stages. Elliot Klayman, Michael Bryan, Dr. Dan Lang, Dr. Daniel Juster, Dr. Walter Riggins, Dr. Donald Carson, and Dr. Michael Schiffman supplied important encouragement at key moments to focus my energies.

I am grateful to Joseph Shulam, leader of a Jerusalem congregation, who wrote the rationale for approaching the scriptures portion-by-portion. His cultural perspective, Hebrew fluency, and life experience add an indigenous expression to authentic Messianic Jewish ways of knowing. Tsvi Sadan gave perspective on the fine balance between scholarly and devotional aspects of the manuscript, as did special friends at Etz Chaim Congregation studying with me through several Torah (*Pentateuch*) cycles. Reb Rez (*Russell Resnik*) played an important role in the selection of Brit Chadashah (*New Testament*) verses to complement the Haftarot (*Prophets and Writings*) that earlier generations of Jews have selected as companion readings to the weekly parashiot (*Scripture portions*).

Intercessors floated my efforts on a cloud of prayer in August, 1997. It made the yoke easy and the burden light. I wrote into the wee hours, enjoying the time. You know who you are. Thank you! Thanks to you all!!   *JEF*

Preface

Jews all over the world gather weekly to read the Torah (*Pentateuch*). They follow a prescribed reading cycle, focusing on a portion of scripture each week. This practice places Jews worldwide literally "on the same page." The calendar of readings commences just after the High Holidays, on the festive day of Simchat Torah (*Joy of the Torah*). Deuteronomy is completed to the cry, "Cha**zak**, cha**zak**, v'nit'cha**zek**! (*Be strong, be strong, & may we be strengthened!*)" Then the scroll is rerolled from end to beginning, and Genesis is chanted afresh: "B'REISHEET (*In the beginning . . .*)

I asked my friend, Joseph Shulam from Jerusalem, about this centuries-old reading practice. He passed along this information about the Parashiot (prescribed *Scripture portions*) and Haftarot (readings from the *Prophets and Writings*) of the Hebrew Bible:

> "Our Bibles today have chapters and verses. This division into chapters and verses was established only in the early part of the sixteenth century. Many centuries before, the Hebrew Pentateuch was divided into parashiot (portions), and these parashiot had companion readings in the Prophetic literature.
>
> The readings from the Prophetic literature were called Haftarot (readings from the Prophets; end, conclusion). These selected readings were paired with the parashiot from the Torah, and read together as literary unities every Shabbat (Sabbath, 7th day).
>
> In the time of the first Temple, the reading of the Torah was divided into 167 portions, called Sedarim (order). The reading of the complete Torah cycle took three-and-a-half years. These Sedarim are marked in the Hebrew Bible with a single samech (the Hebrew letter "S") written on the edge of the page.
>
> The Jews in Babylon consolidated the reading cycle into a one-year cycle. They divided the Torah into

*the 54 "parashiot" which we have today. Each parashah
(portion) is further divided into eight subsections (1st-
rishon, 2nd-sheni, 3rd-shlishi, 4th-r'vi'i, 5th-chamishi,
6th-shishi, 7th-shvi'i, plus the conclusion-maftir).
Maimonides (Rambam) is the earliest source for the present arrangement [Yad haChazakah], but hints can be
seen in Midrash Safra and Sifri, going back to the third
century. In fact, the tradition of reading the Torah every
Sabbath according to some order is evident in Tenach
itself (Neh. 8; Dt. 31:12)."*

Continuing this holy tradition, the Messianic Jewish devotional commentary **Walk GENESIS!** is designed to aid those who
wish to integrate readings from the B'rit Chadashah (*New
Covenant/New Testament*) with the weekly parashiot and haftarot still read by Jewish communities throughout the world.

This study guide assumes that the portion names are not
arbitrary. Rather these names, which always appear within the
first verse or two, carry significant meaning and give forward
movement to the story of God's work to save mankind. Note
how the story unfolds in the Table of Contents. In like manner,
study the titles within each portion to see how the sub-sections
clarify the outline.

One can view Torah as God's revealed blueprint for human
participation in covenant relationship with God. The Haftarah,
then, reflects the prophets' call for us to clean up our act and
return to God's ways. Finally, the B'rit Chadashah describes
how Messiah redeems us and restores our walk down the path
of blessing to everlasting life. Messiah came so you might have
life and have it abundantly (John 10:10b). Begin your journey
now. As you search the scriptures for yourself, God will reveal
His plan and help you walk in this abundance!

*JEF
Simchat Torah, 5758*

Walk GENESIS*!* Features

Each chapter begins with a "doodle" of a scene from the
Torah portion. Embedded in the scene, cursive Hebrew letters
spell out the portion name. Below the "doodle" comes an entertaining synopsis in rhyme. Now on to the meat of the Word!
The facing page has section titles that describe the flow of the
story across the Torah portion, with its related Haftarah and
B'rit Chadashah readings. The key idea of the portion, shown
at the bottom of the page, helps the reader focus.

The *Hiker's Log* offers a cumulative summary of what has
happened to date in the story, a hint at what lies ahead, a box
capsulizing the summary, and a second box listing the people,
places, and events to come.

For Hebrew lovers, *Compass Work* spells out the portion
name letter by letter. Scripture supplies the context for this
name, and the first verse is analyzed phrase by phrase. Related
Words show how the root word gets used in everyday speech.

Each sub-section of Torah then gets featured on a page of its
own, complete with the first verse quoted (last verse for the
maftir to show the seam that concludes the portion). Key ideas
are emphasized, and challenging discussion questions stimulate
searching and contemplation. Please note that the footer at the
bottom of each page references the entire segment under discussion. It is recommended that the reader be familiarized with the
footer segment before reading the commentary on a given page.

The name *Meanderings* suggests how our journey through
Torah now turns to related "excursion side-trips" in the
Haftarah (*Prophets and Writings*) and B'rit Chadashah (*New
Covenant/New Testament*). The format matches that of the Torah
sub-sections. Like the maftir, these pages feature a quote from

the end of passage being studied. Due to the brevity of this section, the reading can become quite demanding. For readers desiring to meditate on these passages, a number of cross-references (cf.) are provided. (***Please note:*** *Selections from the B'rit Chadashah are preliminary efforts to complement the annual reading cycle for the Torah and Haftarah. It is not suggested that the current selections are the only readings or the best readings for a given portion. The author invites readers to suggest alternative selections to improve the quality of this work in future editions.)*

The ***Oasis*** features *Talk Your Walk*, a conclusion drawn from the portion and *Walk Your Talk*, a personal application. Remarks in ***Journey's End*** sum up all of Genesis.

Hebrew names for Torah portions, people, places, and terms of interest are sprinkled throughout the text to add cultural context to the story. The English version and/or meaning generally follows in parentheses; otherwise, check the ***Glossary***. Whenever verse numbers vary, the references for the Tenach are given in parentheses with the Hebrew הנ״ך to identify them.

To use this volume as a daily devotional, the following reading plan is suggested:

Sunday   *Hiker's Log* and *Compass Work* (overview)
Monday   *Rishon (1st)* & *Sheni (2nd)* Sections of the Torah portion
Tuesday   *Shlishi (3rd)* and *R'vi'i (4th)* Sections
Wednesday *Chamishi (5th)* and *Shishi (6th)* Sections
Thursday   *Shvi'i (7th)* and *Maftir (concluding)* Sections
Friday   *Meanderings* (Haftarah and B'rit Chadashah)
Saturday   *Oasis* (summary and application)

Readers with less time might read cross-sectionally, focusing on *Hiker's Log* and *Oasis*—or studying only certain sections each cycle and saving *Meanderings* until foundations are firm.

Table of

Contents

In the beginning, בראשית,
God made heaven 'n earth,
new with life
and new with birth,
with man as the crown
to rule creation,
resting in Eden
for his recreation!

But paradise crashed
'cuz man disobeyed,
and living forever
with God was delayed.
Adam had to die
for his sin to be paid,
but Noach rested
and Noach God saved!

Walk b'Reisheet!
1:1-6:8

בְּרֵאשִׁית

In the beginning

TORAH—Genesis 1:1-6:8
- 1st God Creates—Genesis 1:1
- 2nd A Perfect World—Genesis 2:4
- 3rd Creation's Crown—Genesis 2:20
- 4th God Limits Free Will—Genesis 3:22
- 5th Kayin's Line Pursues Evil—Genesis 4:19
- 6th Be Fruitful, Forever!—Genesis 5:1-2a
- 7th The Line of Shet Continues—Genesis 5:25
- Maftir Noach Finds Grace—Genesis 6:8

HAFTARAH—Isaiah 42:5-43:10
- The Blind Witness—Isaiah 43:10a

B'RIT CHADASHAH—Revelation 22:6-21
- Rest in Grace—Revelation 22:21

*In the Beginning ... God Creates Paradise,
but Man Fails to Rest*

Hiker's Log

 ## Looking Back

We must ask ourselves how we arrived at the present. Scripture says we take our problems with us. Problems left unsolved (e.g. disobedience, sibling rivalry) are transmitted from generation to generation. These problems, recorded in Scripture from the earliest beginnings, explain our world today. For example, Yisra'el's apparent blindness to *"give ear"* (HA'AZINU) to God's way of glorifying Himself among the nations highlights this week's Haftarah (Is. 42:5-43:10).

B'REISHEET (*in the beginning*), before time itself, God creates a perfect world with man as creation's crown. But man disobeys God and eats of the fruit of the Tree of Knowledge to become like God. Now, man can discriminate good from evil. God foresees that man will not attain His predestined purposes, if he eats from the Tree of Life and lives in a fallen state forever. So God banishes Adam (*humankind*) from paradise in Gan Eden.

> *Moshe reminded us,*
> HA'AZINU—*give ear*
> *to God's commands,*
> *leading to this, the blessing—*
> V'ZOT HAB'RACHAH.
> *So ends Deuteronomy and*
> *the yearly cycle of Torah reading.*
> *On Simchat Torah, we roll*
> *the scroll back to Genesis*
> *to begin anew*
> *in the beginning—*B'REISHEET!

Sadly, Adam fails to enter Shabbat (*Sabbath*) rest with God. Man has not completed the work God has given him to do. Instead, Adam's first-born son, Kayin, walks an evil path. Sibling rivalry kindles raging jealousies, leading

Kayin to kill his brother, Hevel. Whereas God curses the ground for Adam's disobedience in Paradise, God curses Kayin for the murder of his brother! Kayin's years are never recorded. In striking contrast, Shet's line (God's *appointed*) fathers children, and their ages are always recorded at fatherhood and at death. The one exception, Chanoch (*disciple*), fathers children, walks with God, and is taken before he dies!

In the tenth generation, **NOACH** (*Noah/rest*) will escape judgment and carry the hope that the fathers can be redeemed! Yeshua warns that the Days of Noach resemble the end of days. Today, people are busy pursuing material prosperity and entertainment apart from God. People say that they are "too busy" to

enter into Shabbat rest. Scripture records these days as times when people are too distracted by life's cares to rest or watch for the coming of Messiah (Mt. 24:37-39). Yet watch we must!

In B'REISHEET...

The Key People include Adam, Chavah (*Eve*), Kayin (*Cain*), Hevel (*Abel*), Chanoch (*Enoch*), Lemech (*Lamech*), Shet (*Seth*), M'tushelach (*Methuselah*), and Noach (*Noah*).

The Scenes include the heavens and earth, Gan Eden (*the Garden of Eden*/Paradise), four rivers—the Pishon, Gichon (*Gihon*), Chidekel (*Tigris*), and F'rat (*Euphrates*), and the land of Nod, east of Eden.

The Main Events include creation, the first Shabbat rest, man's disobedience and the consequences, sons and sacrifices, sibling rivalry, the first murder, and man's wickedness except for Noach.

The Trail Ahead ➡

Compass Work

The Path

בראשית ברא אלהים
את השמים ואת הארץ

—בראשית/א

	ת	י	שׁ	א	רֵ	בְּ
letter:	tav	yod	shin	alef	reish	bet
sound:	T	EE	**SHee**	(silent)	Rei	B'

in the beginning = B'REISHEET = בראשית

The Legend

<u>in the beginning</u>	*b'reisheet*	בְּרֵאשִׁית
created	*bara*	בָּרָא
God	*Elohim*	אֱלֹהִים
— the heavens	*et ha-shamayim*	אֵת הַשָּׁמַיִם
and — the earth	*v'et ha-arets*	וְאֵת הָאָרֶץ:

—*Genesis 1:1*

Related Words

head	*rosh*	רֹאשׁ
New Year (head of the year)	*Rosh haShanah*	רֹאשׁ הַשָּׁנָה
new moon (head of the month)	*Rosh Chodesh*	רֹאשׁ חֹדֶשׁ
first	*rishon*	רִאשׁוֹן
in advance (from the head)	*me-rosh*	מֵרֹאשׁ
head of family (head of fathers)	*rosh avot*	רֹאשׁ אָבוֹת
cornerstone (head of corner)	*rosh pinah*	רֹאשׁ־פִּנָּה
take a census (elevate the head of the people)	*nasa et rosh ha-anashim*	נָשָׂא אֶת רֹאשׁ הָאֲנָשִׁים
mayor (head of the city)	*rosh ha-ir*	רֹאשׁ הָעִיר
tadpole	*roshan*	רֹאשָׁן

Hit the Trail!

God Creates

> ❝ In the beginning God created the heavens and earth. ❞
>
> —*Genesis 1:1*

Before time began, God created space for heaven and earth. God speaks and it happens, but the number seven most stands out! Seven times the Torah reads, "And it was so." Seven times it is recorded, "and God made." Six times God speaks with approval, "Good!" (Gen. 1:4, 10, 12, 18, 21, 25), climaxing the seventh time with "Very Good!" (Gen. 1:31).

The build up to the seventh day is dramatic! Each day of creation ends, "And there was evening and morning, day (one, two, . . . six)."

On the seventh day, God rests; but the account never concludes, "and there was evening and there was morning, day seven." Man's failure to enter Shabbat rest with God on day seven screams out.

God creates and rests, but man fails to enter Shabbat rest with God.

Thus, the rishon *(first)* section of B'REISHEET leaves the beginning open-ended. The next verse, (Genesis 2:4), begins the creation account anew—but this time from the perspective of man!

Re-read the seven times God says ki-tov (that it's good). Notice that God does not say ki-tov after day two. Why do you suppose God walls off heaven with a barrier, ends the day, but does not say "Good!" for that day's work?

A Perfect World

❝ Here is the history of the heavens and the earth when they were created. On the day when ADONAI, God, made earth and heaven . . . ❞

—Genesis 2:4

Perspective shifts! The first account starts with the literal words *"in beginning"* and has an absolute sense which comes before time. Here, the perspective changes from creating to literally *"the making of earth and heaven."* Commenting on Gen. 1:14, Rashi says that everything was created (in potential) on the first day, but the actual generating takes place on the days that follow.

Thus, the tol'dot (*generations, life story, offspring*) of the universe (Gen. 2:4) describe the generating of life in the context of heaven and earth. Here, the sequence of creation takes a back seat to the drama surrounding God's purposes for man and his being placed in Gan Eden (*paradise*).

> ### God places man in Gan Eden to do meaningful work.

God commands man not to eat from the Tree of the Knowledge of Good and Evil. Man is told to care for the garden, to eat freely from its fruits, and to order creation by naming all living creatures.

> *On day 3, God says "Good!" twice—once after the waters are gathered and once after herbs and greens sprout on the dry land that appears. Explain what is "Good!" about creating the Trees of Life and Knowledge.*

Creation's Crown

> ❝ *So the person gave names to all the livestock, to the birds in the air and to every wild animal. But for Adam there was not found a companion suitable for helping him.* ❞
> —Genesis 2:20

Man "called names" to all the cattle, birds, and beasts. Later, the LORD will "call" (VAYIKRA) a priesthood from "the names" (SH'MOT) of those who go down to Egypt to become a nation.

> **Man, as crown, orders creation by naming.**

Here, man "calls names" to the animals in Gan Eden. Man's work is to order creation. Naming involves asserting authority (Gen. 1:26, 28). God assigns names to the celestials (heaven, earth, seas, darkness, day and night); now, man orders the terrestrials by naming the animals, fulfilling the command to rule over every living creature (Gen. 1:28). Man is the crown of creation—higher than any other terrestrial, and only a little lower than angels in the heavenly order.

But a helpmate is missing. All animals have a partner, but man has none. The LORD creates woman, his complement, as a sustainer beside him (Gen. 2:20, 3:20), and man names her Chavah (*mother of the living*).

> ❓ *God speaks and creates the universe. Now man speaks and names the animals. In what way is the LORD assigning man the kind of work that is in His own image? Explain the saying, "Your word is your bond."*

God Limits Free Will

❝ ADONAI, God, said, "See, the man has become like one of us, knowing good and evil. Now, to prevent his putting out his hand and taking also from the tree of life, eating, and living forever" ❞ —Gen. 3:22

Man chooses to disobey God and eat of the fruit of the Tree of the Knowledge of Good and Evil. Immediately, he becomes separated from terrestrials, knowing good and evil. God banishes him from Gan Eden, lest he eat from the Tree of Life and spend eternity seeking sensual gratification.

Because man disobeys, the LORD limits his access to eternal life.

Jewish commentators say that man's enhanced desire for sensual gratification competes with God's intended spiritual bliss [Rambam, Sforno]. Man loses access to the Tree of Life (cf. Gen. 2:9, 16-17). God intervenes to drive man from Paradise, lest man eat of the Tree of Life and pursue sensual gratification forever.

The ground is cursed and man must struggle by the sweat of his brow for the food he needs to live (Gen. 3:19, cf. 2:15). Lost is man's immediate access to the Presence of God. Man must die—return to the adamah (*ground*) as a consequence of the knowledge he has gained.

? • Do you think a life of study of God's Word, prayer, and self-discipline can curb man's appetites for selfishness, lust, and greed? Can basic human nature be transformed in this life? Is there a way to restore healthy appetites?

Kayin's Line Pursues Evil

> ❝ Lemekh took himself two wives; the name of the one was 'Adah, while the name of the other was Tzilah. ❞
>
> —Genesis 4:19

Lemech has the curious distinction of being the first recorded bigamist. According to Rashi, Lemech fathers and later kills his son, Tuval-Kayin.

It was common for the generation living in the days of Noach to keep one wife for children and another wife for pleasure [Rashi]. The wife that was for pleasure was pampered; the other wife was often ignored.

Here, both wives bear children. Note that Adah means *ornamented* or *pretty*. Adah's firstborn, Yaval, becomes father of those who wander with herds (Gen. 4:20, cf. Gen. 4:16, where Kayin goes eastward to Nod, an area east of Eden meaning *wandering* or *exile*).

Lemech, a bigamist in the days of Noach, ends Kayin's line.

Torah does not record the ages of Kayin or any of the sons in Kayin's line (Gen. 4:17-22), contrasting sharply with those in Shet's line, whose ages are given when they first become fathers and again when they die (Gen. 5:1-32) or "walk with" God (5:22-24).

? Note that Shet's great-great-great-great-great-grandson fathers Noach, survivor and father of mankind, whereas Kayin's great-great-great-grandson perishes, never to father again. Read Mt. 24:38-40. Can man father sons forever?

Be Fruitful, Forever!

❝ Here is the genealogy of Adam. On the day that God created man he made him in the likeness of God; he created them male and female; he . . . called them Adam [humankind, man] . . . ❞—Gen. 5:1-2a

Both male and female are created in the likeness of God. Adam also becomes the personal name of the man (Gen. 5:3). However, God first calls both male and female "Adam" (humankind). No stronger statement can be made about the spiritual co-equality of male and female.

The man apart from the woman is incomplete.

The continuity of Adam, as mankind, can only be assured by the cleaving of ish (*man*) and ishah (*woman*) as one flesh (Gen. 2:24). Mankind is incomplete apart from the joining together of both man and woman.

The blessing of fruitfulness follows a familiar pattern with firstborns living to father firstborns, and then living some more, fathering sons and daughters. Fathers die after that, but the next firstborn continues the toldot (*generations*). In this segment, the pattern culminates in Chanoch, a firstborn who fathers the oldest man in the world, before God takes him alive!

The Zohar says that the soul descends from heaven and has two parts, male and female. These become separated and enter different bodies. Relate this to the idea that "all marriages are made in heaven." Is singleness incomplete?

The Line of Shet Continues

> **"** *Metushelach lived 187 years and fathered Lemekh.* **"**
>
> *—Genesis 5:25*

The oldest man in Torah fathers a son named Lemech. M'tushelach will then live another 782 years—outliving his son (cf. Adam), watching his grandson Noach build the ark (for 120 years), and dying in 1656, the year of the flood.

The fathers die, but some of the sons live on.

All the fathers in the ten generations from Adam (through Shet) to Noach live, father sons, then live some more, and die (*va-yamot*)—except Chanoch. He "walks with" God and escapes death (Heb. 7:14). The fathers, first-borns, and life spans follow:

Adam	*0-930*
Shet	*130-1042*
Enosh	*235-1140*
Keinan	*325-1235*
Mahalal'el	*395-1290*
Yered	*460-1422*
Chanoch	*622-987*
M'tushelach	*687-1656*
Lemech	*874-1651*
Noach	*1056-*

Both Shet and Kayin father sons named Lemech, but only one passes on a father-to-son heritage to his son.

? *The Rabbis say that only when a man is united with his wife can he be called "adam"—otherwise he is an "ish" [Yev. 63a]. The line of Kayin died in the flood. Can mankind live forever by passing a heritage to his sons?*

Noach Finds Grace

❝ But Noach found grace in the sight of ADONAI. ❞
—*Genesis 6:8*

The LORD determines to blot out man from the record (Ex. 17:14; 32:33-34). Fewer people than a minyan (*ten*) will survive. In fact, only Noach finds chen (*grace, favor*) in God's sight.

Humankind saddens God by choosing to walk in evil ways, not in good.

Noach is the first man born after Adam dies. His father gives him a name that welcomes the easing of man's struggle for survival expected as a result of Adam's death [Gen. 3:18-19; 5:29, Abarbanel].

Noach's chen refers to a situation where a superior helps one without status (Gen. 39:4; Ex. 33:17). Here, the whole of humankind faces the consequences of introducing the knowledge of evil into the world. Such knowledge includes sorrow, suffering, and ultimately death.

In the face of this bleak news, God has appointed Shet (*Seth/appointed*) to replace Hevel (*Abel/transitory*), taken Chanoch (*Enoch/disciple*) before he dies, and now graciously redeems Noach (*Noah/rest*) from the fruits of mankind's evil direction.

Read Ez. 14:13-14. Though Noach's sons and their wives are not called righteous, God showed grace by saving them anyway. Can you explain divine justice? Why did God save them and not others too? (Read Ac. 16:31; Ro. 11:26.)

Meander

❝ *"You are my witnesses," says ADONAI, "and my servant whom I have chosen, so that you can know and trust me and understand that I am he . . ."* ❞

—*Isaiah 43:10a*

The passage begins with the creation account (Is. 42:5), advancing quickly to Yisra'el's role as mediator of a covenant to all mankind and light to the nations (Is. 42:6). The LORD convenes a court and assembles the nations for a trial (Is. 43:8-9). Who is God, Master Creator and LORD of the nations? The idols of the nations have no witnesses or prophets to interpret. All are silent. They cannot explain the rise of Koresh (*Cyrus, king of Persia*) as God's anointed.

God summons Yisra'el. Alas! Yisra'el is deaf and blind! (Is. 42:19). But God, who created the heavens and formed Yisra'el from the beginning, has redeemed her (Is. 43:1-3). Pharaoh's son has paid the price for Yisra'el's ransom (Is. 43:4; Ex. 4:22-23).

The blind and deaf servant witnesses that God preserves His people.

Deaf and blind from the effects of sin, Yisra'el is led into court in the presence of the nations. Can Yisra'el be shamed (Is. 42:17) into realizing chesed (*God's covenant kindness*)? God exclaims to Yisra'el, "You are my witnesses" (Is. 43:10)!

❓ *Read Is. 59:21. Comment on God's use of Yisra'el as His witness despite her sins. Compare Yisra'el's fallen state (Is. 42) with her restoration (Is. 43). How does God use Peter and those praying for him as His blind servants? (Ac. 12)*

...ings

> **"** *May the grace of the Lord Yeshua be with all!* **"**
> —*Revelation 22:21*

The rest which Adam fails to enter, the fathers of Yisra'el also fail to enter (Heb. 3:17)—due to unbelief and deliberate disobedience (Ps. 95:10; Num. 14:23, 29-30, 35). God swears the fathers will not enter His rest, even though He Himself has rested (Gen.2:2; Ex. 31:17).

God's rest is offered again to Yisra'el under Y'hoshua (Josh. 21:44; 22:4, 23:1; note Dt. 12:9-10), under David (Ps. 95:6-8, 11), and then under Yeshua (Mt. 11:28-30).

The Shabbat rest of God is still available today (Heb. 4:8-9). One must hasten to flee intelligent, planned unbelief, since listening without ears of faith leads to hardening of the heart (Heb. 4:1,2; 3:13).

Believers must actively hasten to appropriate the grace of God.

Those who are consecrated must hasten to enter the rest of God (Heb. 4:11), because He is coming soon (Rev. 22:7, 12, 20). Believers are called to appropriate, responding quickly and actively to God's call. "Come, Lord Yeshua. Come!!" Amen.

? *What work did Yeshua hasten before He rested? (Jn. 13:27; Mt. 26:41, 45). Striving to rest sounds like a contradiction, but hard work assures a good night's sleep. How should man hasten to enter into the grace of God? (Gen. 6:7-8)*

Oasis

Talk Your Walk . . .

In the beginning, God created heaven and earth as a paradise, with man as the crown to oversee creation. God gave man meaningful work—to name the animals and oversee their function in the order of creation. This work required man to discern the nature of all creation and to participate in the work of God on earth as a fellow co-creator. Indeed, Paradise is a curse-free place, and the "work" of it is a restful activity to be shared with the LORD Himself.

In the beginning, God creates perfection . . . but man fails to enter.

But man failed to enter the rest of God (Gen. 2:2; Heb. 4:4). Man never said, "It is finished!" As a result, Scripture never writes, "And there was evening and morning, the seventh day." Unlike the previous six days of creation, day seven never ends. Yet Shabbat rest comes at the journey's end!

One can speculate why God said, "Good!" after each day's work except for day two (when He built a firmament to wall off heaven from earth). Did God reserve heaven for His abode, so that He could rest even if man chose to scurry around chasing after evil desires?

. . . Walk Your Talk

Believers are called to enter into the sabbatismos (*rest*) of God (Heb. 4:9). What makes this rest so elusive for man? How did Adam, and Yisra'el's generation of fathers in the wilderness, fail to enter the rest of God? And why is this rest so difficult for believers to appropriate in their personal quiet times today? Most certainly we are told that there remains a Shabbat rest for the people of God (Heb. 4:9). And just as surely as God finished His work and entered His rest (Gen. 2:2), so we are encouraged to follow in like manner (Heb. 4:10). Yeshua, as the Son of Man, showed us how!

As He lay dying on the cross as the Passover lamb of God, Yeshua ended His work with the words, "It is finished!" (Jn. 19:30). He gave up His spirit shortly before the full moon of the first month's Shabbat (*Sabbath*). And He lay in the ground for a little of day six, a little of day eight (before dawn), but the whole of the Shabbat.

> *When our work is finished, we can enter Shabbat rest with God.*

Thus, He rested for three different days, but the whole Shabbat. And then He was redeemed as the firstfruits from those who are sleeping (1 Cor. 15:20). Yeshua rested, and God redeemed Him forevermore.

Shabbat Shalom!

Now נֹחַ means
"the one who rests"
with his sons and the animals
on water crests.
In the ark they lived
and passed all the tests—
the lambs laid down
on the lions' breasts.

So God made a covenant
saying, "Never again!"
would He blot out all life
to slay evil men.
He promised to live
in the tents of Shem
and to bless mankind
as His special friend!

Walk NOACH!
6:9-11:32

Noah (rest)

TORAH—Genesis 6:9-11:32
- 1st Noach & Sons—Genesis 6:9
- 2nd Enter the Ark!—Genesis 7:1
- 3rd Mankind Swamped!—Genesis 7:17
- 4th Noach's House Saved—Genesis 8:15-17
- 5th God Covenants—Genesis 9:8-10a
- 6th The Noach-Shem Connection—Genesis 9:18
- 7th Making of the Nations—Genesis 11:1
- Maftir Idolater Cut Off—Genesis 11:32

HAFTARAH—Isaiah 54:1-55:5
- David-Yisra'el Connection—Isaiah 55:5

B'RIT CHADASHAH—Matthew 24:36-47
- Faithful Servant Inherits!—Matthew 24:46-47

Noach Rests while
Mankind Gets Swamped

Hiker's Log

 Looking Back

God creates heaven and earth as a paradise B'REISHEET (*in the beginning*), and He crowns man with authority to oversee creation. But man determines to be like God—able to distinguish good from evil. Adam's firstborn son, Kayin, kills his brother. God uproots Kayin from his farming way of life and forces him to wander without rest in Nod (a land whose name means *wandering* in exile). Kayin's sons father sons, but their ages are never recorded—neither when they father children nor when they die. Imagine their gravestones, without the date of birth or the date of death.

After seven generations, Lemech is born—history's first adulterer. Jewish tradition ascribes the death of Kayin and Tuval-Kayin (Lemech's son) to Lemech. The fruits of evil are made abundantly clear: the murderer and the adulterer walk an evil path, and neither will inherit eternal life. Kayin is cursed by God for murdering Hevel, his brother. Ultimately, his entire line perishes.

> *We began in the beginning—*
> **B'REISHEET!**
> *Out of chaos, order.*
> *All things perfect.*
> *But men failed to rest . . .*
> *all except* **NOACH.**

In contrast, Shet is *appointed* to take Hevel's place. In the seventh generation, Chanoch walks with God, fathers a different Lemech in the Shet line and others, and then is taken by God just after Adam's death. The picture of everyone from Shet to Lemech watching as Chanoch is taken brings indescribable hope to humankind! Lemech bears **NOACH** (*Noah/rest*) saying, "He will bring us relief . . . from the ground the LORD has cursed" (Gen. 5:29). Adam's death is expected to bring atonement, relief from the accursed toil required to bring forth fruit from the ground.

Noach follows in the path of Chanoch as a "righteous-blameless," a son who enters fatherhood and escapes the wrath of God's judgment on mankind. Noach becomes the first son to father sons who also live to father sons. This pattern contrasts sharply with Adam's generations, where the fathers die and Adam sees neither Chanoch taken nor Noach born. Both Noach and his son, Shem, live to see

In NOACH . . .

The Key People include Noach (*Noah*), Shem, Cham (*Ham*), Yefet (*Japheth*), their wives, C'na'an (*Canaan*), Terach (*Terah*), Avram (*Abram*), Nachor (*Nahor*), Haran, Lot, Sarai, and Milcah.

The Scenes include the mountains of Ararat, plains of Shin'ar (*Shinar*), Ur Casdim (*Ur of the Chaldeans*), and Charan (*Haran*).

The Main Events include the ark, flood, covenant, rainbow, vineyard fiasco, Shem's blessing, Tower of Bavel (*Babel*), and Terach's move.

Avram (the hope of redemption) fathered in the tenth generation!

Terach is the only father listed in Noach's line to father a son "and die." He does not forsake idolatry—small wonder he dies cut off from the eternal rest given to his son, Avraham, in the Land.

The Trail Ahead ➡

Compass Work

The Path

אֵלֶּה תּוֹלְדֹת נֹחַ
נֹחַ אִישׁ צַדִּיק
תָּמִים הָיָה בְּדֹרֹתָיו
אֶת הָאֱלֹהִים הִתְהַלֶּךְ נֹחַ

—בראשית ו/ ט

	חַ	נֹ
letter:	chet	nun
sound:	aCH	**No**

 *Noah (rest)* = NOACH = נֹחַ

The Legend

these (are)	*eleh*	אֵלֶּה
generations of <u>Noah</u>	*tol'dot <u>Noach</u>*	תּוֹלְדֹת נֹחַ
<u>Noah</u> (was)	*<u>Noach</u>*	נֹחַ
man righteous	*eesh tsadik*	אִישׁ צַדִּיק
perfect he was	*tamim hayah*	תָּמִים הָיָה
in generations-of-his	*b'dorotav*	בְּדֹרֹתָיו
— God	*et-ha-Elohim*	אֶת־הָאֱלֹהִים
<u>Noah</u> walked with	*hit'halech-<u>Noach</u>*	הִתְהַלֶּךְ־נֹחַ:

—*Genesis 6:9*

Related Words

restful, quiescent	*nach*	נָח
convenient, congenial, easy-going, pleasant	*noach*	נוֹחַ
to rest, lie down, repose, settle down	*nuach*	נוּחַ
deceased (resting soul)	*nuach nefesh*	נוּחַ נֶפֶשׁ
May he rest in Paradise!	*nucho Eden*	נוּחוֹ עֵדֶן
comfortable life	*chayim nochim*	חַיִּים נוֹחִים
convenience, comfort	*nochoot*	נוֹחוּת
to be inspired (rested upon him the spirit)	*nachah alav ruach*	נָחָה עָלָיו רוּחַ

Hit the Trail!

Noach & Sons

> ❝ *Here is the history of Noach. In his generation, Noach was a man righteous and wholehearted; Noach walked with God.* ❞
>
> —*Genesis 6:9*

Noach and Chanoch are described as righteous-blameless men who walk with God. Chanoch is "taken," and Noach becomes the only father to live through the flood. Noach survives, because he obeys God and builds an ark, exactly as God had commanded him (Gen. 6:22).

Kayin's line perishes completely in the flood, with Lemech outliving his son, Tubal-Kayin, whom he kills [Rashi; cf. Adam and Hevel].

In contrast, Shet's line is preserved: Chanoch is taken, and his son, another Lemech, fathers Noach, the first father to live on when God judges humankind.

The father and all his sons are saved from judgment.

A picture of redemption emerges. Adam fathers three sons, but only the "appointed" one survives. Noach fathers three sons, and all of them survive. In fact, Shem will live to see the birth of Ya'akov, father of a nation!

> **?** *The corporate prayers of Yisra'el (such as Kaddish and the Sh'ma) require a minyan (10 or more). Explain whether or not Adam (head of humankind) perishes in the flood. Does Adam live through his son Noach or not?*

Enter the Ark!

> ❝ ADONAI *said to Noach, "Come into the ark, you and all your household; for I have seen that you alone in this generation are righteous before me.* ❞
> —Genesis 7:1

Bo! (*Enter!*)—you and your household. The LORD uses this same word (Ex. 10:1) to direct Moshe to "enter into" negotiations with Par'oh (*Pharaoh*) to redeem the sons of Yisra'el from oppression in Egypt.

The LORD shows grace to Noach and his family, too.

Here, Noach alone is described as righteous (Gen. 7:1). Yet God directs him to save his sons and their wives. God's chen (*grace*) toward Noach is evident in the saving of his household. This grace is foundational to the saving of all Yisra'el as a nation out of Egypt and to the promise that all Yisra'el will be saved at the end of time (Ro. 11:26).

We are told M'tushelach dies in the year of the flood, and the final week is needed to complete shiv-ah (*seven-day mourning period*) [Rashi]. God waits the final week (Gen. 7:4), and then He lovingly shuts Noach and his family into the ark (Gen. 7:16). No other father in the line from Adam to Noach is still living at the time of the flood.

❓ *Read Dan. 9:27; Mt. 24:15-22, 37-38. God personally seals those who receive grace into the ark one week before the flood. Explain the relationship between the final week in the Days of Noach and Daniel's seventieth week.*

Mankind Swamped!

❝ The flood was forty days on the earth; the water grew higher and floated the ark, so that it was lifted up off the earth. ❞

—Genesis 7:17

Waters pour forth, from the heavens above, but also from t'hom (*the deep*) [Sifrei Chachamim, Mizrachi].

Waters pour forth from the heavens and from the deep.

When Torah is sung, the chanting marks (*darga-t'vir* combination) under the words "and there was the flood" lend a "from above" and "from beneath" pulsing rhythm. One can almost feel the waters surging! The waters rise from the deep for another 150 days, even after the rains end (Gen. 7:18-19, 24), before cresting and then receding (Gen. 8:3).

The waters of the deep multiply, lifting the ark to safety, but creating chaos and judging all life on earth! (Gen. 7:17, 22; cf. Gen. 1:28). All earth—even Mt. Ararat, the highest point—is submerged under 22-30 feet of water. The judgment lasts exactly one year (Gen. 7:11, 8:13-14; the solar year is eleven days longer that the lunar year).

? *Read Prov. 11:31 and Gen. 7:23. Rashi says that the righteous one receives retribution for his sins while he is still on earth. Explain whether or not Noach and the flood gives corporate humankind a cleansed, fresh start.*

Noach's House Saved

> ❝ God said to Noach, "Go out from the ark, you, your wife, your sons and your sons' wives with you. Bring out with you every living thing . . . " ❞
>
> —Genesis 8:15-17

Exit! The LORD tells Noach, his wife, his sons, and their wives to exit the ark (Gen. 8:15).

God commands living creatures to fill the earth.

In a later portion, VAYETSE Ya'akov (*and Jacob went out*) from his parents' home to escape Esav's wrath and start a household (Gen. 28:10). This household will grow to 70 people, journey to Egypt, and become a nation to reach the nations of the world. Here, Noach's household exits the ark and soon multiplies to become the 70 nations of the world.

But first, the entire sequence of creation is repeated. To stop the flood, the deep is closed (Gen. 8:2, cf. Gen. 1:2, 6). Then the dry ground appears and the ark rests (Gen. 8:4, cf. Gen. 1:9). Next, God commands all life to "teem" upon the earth (Gen. 8:17, cf. Gen. 1:20, 22). Finally, God commands the people to multiply upon the earth (Gen. 9:1, 7, cf. Gen. 1:28).

? *Did God fail to say "good" when He walled off the "waters above" on day two because He foresaw using these waters to judge the earth? Explain why the days of creation are reenacted in the Noach story. How about day 4?*

God Covenants

> **❝** *God spoke to Noach and his sons with him; he said, "As for me—I am herewith establishing my covenant with you, with your descendants after you, and with every living creature . . .* **❞** *—Gen. 9:8-10a*

The Noachide covenant is God's flat promise never to destroy His creation by flood (Gen. 9:11-13). Many take this to mean that never again will God destroy creation [Or HaChaim], even if man is sinful [Chizkuni].

God covenants never again to destroy all the earth.

Parallels suggest redemptive continuities between Adam and Noach as patriarchal figures or fathers of humankind. Both are created in God's image (Gen. 1:27; 9:6), and both are commanded to be fruitful, multiply, father creation, fill the earth, and rule over it (Gen. 1:28; 9:1-2).

Man's requirement to walk in covenant relationship is spelled out in the Noachide (Noachian) Laws, which preceded the giving of Torah and are reaffirmed in the B'rit Chadashah [Ac. 15:20, 28-32; Gen. 9:3-6; Sanh. 56a]. Halachah (*Hebrew law*) affirms that Christians and Muslims who keep the Noachide laws will inherit a share in the world to come [Tosef. Sanh. 13:2].

> **?** *Review Gen. 9:13, 16-17. To whom is the rainbow given as a sign of the covenant? On day four, God creates the luminaries as signs to mark off His order (Gen. 1:14). Explain God's promise to all living creatures of the earth.*

The Noach-Shem Connection

> **"** *The sons of Noach who went out from the ark were Shem, Ham and Yefet. Ham is the father of Kena'an.* **"**
>
> —*Genesis 9:18*

Shem is not the firstborn, but he is first to obey God's order to emerge from the ark. Cham (*Ham*) is curiously introduced as the father of C'na'an. Torah emphasizes this insight by stating it twice (Gen. 9:18, 22).

> ### Noach fathers three sons, who become seventy nations.

Seventy primary nations, the nations of the earth, are fathered by Noach's three sons: Yefet's nations (Europe) number 14, Shem's nations (Asia) number 26, and Cham's nations (Africa) number 30, including the accursed C'na'anim (Gen. 9:25).

Rashi writes that Shem's righteousness places him first among the sons [Gen. 5:32; Br. R. 26:3], though Yefet is likely the eldest [Gen. 10:21; Maskil l'David]. Sforno notes in Gen. 10:21 a double meaning for Shem's role as "avi kol b'nei-Ever." Shem not only *fathers all sons from across* the river. He is also *father of the sons of Ever*, passing on fatherly wisdom and a heritage to those soon to become the Ivrim (*Hebrews*) [Sforno, p.56].

? *Fathers teach sons, and sons learn to walk after their fathers (Gen. 4:20-21; 1 Sam. 10:12; 1 Ki. 20:35). Is Avraham the first monotheist, or did he learn about God from something Noach first taught Shem?*

The Making of the Nations

> " *The whole earth used the same language, the same words.* "
>
> —*Genesis 11:1*

Bavel, in Iraq, is where the world concentrated its forces [Rashi]. We are told that all nations spoke Hebrew then, the same language God spoke when He created the world [Mizrachi].

The nations attempt to build a tower as a rallying point for piercing heaven, to dethrone God and make a shem (*name*) for themselves. Noach and Shem, eyewitnesses to the flood, are summarily ignored, along with God's command to spread throughout the earth (Gen. 9:1, 19).

God descends (Gen. 11:5), determined to break the unity and hasten the scattering process through balal (*confusion*) of the language, so the nations hear one another's words as bavel (*babble*).

God invents languages to divide humankind.

Noach blesses Shem, saying C'na'an will be his servant and Yefet will dwell in the tents of Shem (Gen. 9:26-27). These words are soon to be fulfilled in a big way by the Almighty Himself.

? *Read Jn. 17:20-23. Yeshua's final prayer for all believers (including those yet to be born!) requests the same unity as the LORD and Yeshua share from the beginning of time. Explain why God divided humankind when unity is the goal.*

Idolater Cut Off

> **❝** *Terach lived 205 years, and he died in Haran.* **❞**
> —Genesis 11:32

Terach's death at 205 closes out the portion detailing the life of Noach. A new era begins when God calls Avram.

Terach is actually 145 when Avram is commanded by God to go forth from his father's house (70+75 years; cf. Gen. 12:4 and Gen. 11:26). Avraham leaves immediately, dying spiritually to Terach—even as Terach dies spiritually to God by keeping his idols at Charan (*the crossroads*) and not completing the journey to the Promised Land.

All patriarchal figures from Noach to Avram are living in 1948, the year of Avram's birth. But Noach, Peleg, and Nachor do not witness Avram's walk of faith in the year 2023:

Noach	(1056-2006)
Shem	(1558-2158)
Arpachshad	(1658-2096)
Shelach	(1693-2126)
Ever	(1723-2187)
Peleg	(1757-1996)
R'u	(1787-2026)
S'rug	(1819-2049)
Nachor	(1849-1997)
Terach	(1878-2083)

Terach dies, cut off spiritually from Avram.

Avram	(1948-).

? *Terach lives in the nineteenth generation from Adam. Is it mere coincidence that the nation of Yisra'el has 19 idolatrous kings before it is cut off from the land? What unsolved problems make Samaria "occupied territory" today?*

Meander

❝ You will summon a nation you do not know, and a nation that doesn't know you will run to you, for the sake of ADONAI your God, the Holy One of Isra'el, who will glorify you. ❞   —Isaiah 55:5

Great joy and jubilation are destined for Tsiyon (*Zion*)! No more will she be exiled, reduced in numbers, and forsaken by the LORD (Is. 54:1).

The LORD is still married (Is. 54:5), and He would never disown Yisra'el, whom He compares to the wife of one's youth (Is. 54:6). "Briefly I abandoned you" (Is. 54:7), but "just as I swore that no flood like Noach's would ever again cover the earth, so now I swear that never again will I be angry with you or rebuke you" (Is. 54:9).

The LORD envisions a glorious Y'rushalayim (*Jerusalem*), with foundations, pinnacles, gates, and walls of precious stones (Is. 54:11-12; Rev. 21:9-27). He Himself will personally teach all children of Tsiyon (Is. 54:13; Jn. 6:45).

The Holy One has glorified Yisra'el!

The covenant of a dynasty and kingdom among nations now becomes the sacred heritage of Yisra'el among the nations! (Is. 55:4-5).

❓ David committed adultery and murder (2 Sam. 11:1-27; 12:9), but God redeems him with mercy (2 Sam 12:13-24).
● Here, God extends the covenant to Yisra'el. Explain how this covenant includes the Messiah and all who believe.

...ings

> 66 "... It will go well with that servant if he is found doing his job when his master comes. Yes, I tell you that he will put him in charge of all he owns..." 99
> —Matthew 24:46-47

The unexpectedness of the coming of Messiah is stated most clearly! "But when that day and hour will come, no one knows—not the angels in heaven, not the Son, only the Father" (Mt. 24:36).

Those who dismiss Yeshua's return by saying He delays are listening to an evil heart (Mt. 24:48). Be warned! If you decide to eat and drink with drunkards, you will be cut in two—as an animal is sacrificed to institute a covenant (Ex. 29:17-18). With weeping and gnashing of teeth, you will sorrow for eternity (Mt. 24:51).

Remember, the flood came unexpectedly and caught many by surprise, except the vigilant Noach (Mt. 24:37-42). So also, the second coming will catch many. Therefore, be ready all the time.

The faithful servant watches vigilantly.

The LORD will set the faithful and vigilant servant over all his property—blessed is that servant (Mt. 24:43-47)!

> ? To be blessed with the promises of David requires vigilance. In what way do you live today watching for Yeshua's return? How can you better prepare yourself?

Oasis

Talk Your Walk . . .

Noach's generation lives through its sons—in stark contrast to Adam's generation which fathers sons and then dies out. Noach becomes the patriarch of mankind who begins the spiritual journey to enter God's rest. This journey includes repopulating the earth, spawning the 70 nations, and redeeming the land. Lemech (in the line of Adam and Shet), names his son Noach, saying, "This one will comfort us in our labor . . . [to get what comes] from the ground that ADONAI cursed" (Gen. 5:28).

> *Noach's household is saved from the judgment on all mankind.*

Then, in an act of unmerited grace, Noach (with his household!) enters the ark and rests. Earth is judged and cleansed—the deep swallows up all murderers and adulterers. God covenants, with a rainbow as a reminder, never again to destroy all life.

Though not the oldest son, Shem is first to exit the ark. Whereas mankind unites against God to make a name for itself in Shin'ar at the Tower of Bavel, God builds upon the Noach-Shem connection to launch His own initiative on earth through Noach's tenth generational son Avram, the "exalted father," soon to be renamed Avraham, "the father of a mass of nations." But first the portion cuts off with the death of Avram's father Terach—an idolater and the only father of Noach's generation to die (Gen. 11:32).

. . . Walk Your Talk

Can you believe that God created the world so man could rest with Him in paradise? It is a lofty thought to consider yourself the crown of creation. You are more blessed than you believe. Perhaps you lose sight of this thought as you compare yourself to others, or when you think you are not good enough. Yet low self-esteem insults your Creator! He created you to suit His purposes. Do you know God's purposes for your life?

Man's disobedience seems to have dethroned man from his lofty beginnings. This disobedience led directly to God's

> *God blesses the man who enters His rest.*

curse upon the ground. Making a living is tough to do. The sweat of one's brow is pure sweat!

But Lemech named Noach, because his son's life led to an easing of the curse. Since then, God has covenanted with Noach to bless mankind to increase in numbers and master all creation. Man now numbers over 5.5 billion—and the increase has been steadily upward, despite the Tower of Bavel, the fall of Babylon, the Temple, Rome, and the destruction of world war. In what ways are you working with God to redeem a world in exile from Paradise?

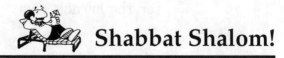 **Shabbat Shalom!**

Now God said to Avram,
"לֶךְ לְךָ!"
Go from your country!
Go from your pa!
Your name will be known
and your household, too.
Just believe in Me,
and watch what I'll do!

You'll father a son
when you're ninety-nine.
Every nation will be blessed
by your family line.
So from scratch
Avi's family was begun,
as they waited in faith
for the miracle son!

Walk LECH L'CHA!
12:1-17:27

Go forth, yourself!

TORAH—Genesis 12:1-17:27
- 1st Go Start a Household!—Genesis 12:1
- 2nd Not in Egypt—Genesis 12:14
- 3rd Not in Jordan—Genesis 13:5-6a
- 4th Not in Shin'ar—Genesis 14:1-2a
- 5th Not in S'dom—Genesis 14:21
- 6th In the Promised Land—Genesis 15:7
- 7th In Covenant Relationship—Genesis 17:7
- Maftir An International Household—Genesis 17:26-27

HAFTARAH—Isaiah 40:27-41:16
- Stronger than Nations—Isaiah 41:16

B'RIT CHADASHAH—Romans 4:1-25
- A Heavenly Inheritance—Romans 4:24b-25

Go Forth, Yourself,
and Walk in Faith, Avraham!

Hiker's Log

God creates a paradise b'REISHEET (*in the beginning*), and He crowns man to oversee creation. But man determines to be like God, able to distinguish good from evil. Adam's firstborn, Kayin, kills Hevel, his brother. Hevel is replaced by Shet, whom God *appoints*.

> **B'REISHEET**—*in the beginning, paradise! But we wouldn't rest . . . only* **NOACH** *walked with God. After the flood, we grabbed for heaven at Bavel. Now, redemption rests in a new man and his family. Go forth, yourself, Avram—* **LECH L'CHA!!!**

Although Adam never sees Chanoch taken, Shet and all his descendants do, including Lemech in the ninth generation. All b'nei adam (*sons of Adam*) glimpse resurrection hope from afar when they see Chanoch escape death. Still, Shet dies with the fathers, whereas **NOACH** (*Noah/rest*) is redeemed as the only father to escape judgment along with his household.

Noach's household is saved by the LORD's grace to adam (*humankind*). Noach becomes the first son to live on as a father and see ten generations. The scriptural phrase *and he died* highlights the fact that Chanoch did not die in the line from Adam to Noach; it also highlights the fact that Terach died, in the tol'dot (*generations*) from Noach to Avram.

The idol maker, Terach, dies at Charan (*the crossroads*). He is cut off from his son, Avram, and never enters the Land. Meanwhile, Avram, *the exalted father*, is destined to become *father to a mass of nations* with a new name, Avraham. Those with

Avram (Sarai, Lot, even his foreign-born household) prosper, get circumcised, enter an everlasting covenant, and beget nations which live on.

Through nations, fathers hope to pass on an everlasting heritage of land and seed to the generations that follow. At the flood, judgment dashes Kayin's hopes for such a heritage. No murderer, idolater, or adulterer shall inherit eternal life (1 Jn. 3:15; 1 Cor. 6:9).

In tol'dot Noach (*the generations of Noah*), all fathers live on through their children. Progress in redemption will demand that the sons escape death by hoping to obtain God's chen (*favor*).

"**Lech l'Cha** (*Go forth, yourself!*)," says the Lord—commanding Avram to leave his land, his birthplace, and

In Lech l'Cha . . .

The Key People include Avram (*Abram*), Sarai, Lot, Par'oh (*Pharaoh*), king of Shin'ar, king of S'dom (*Sodom*), Melchi-Tsedek (*Melchizedek*), Eli'ezer, Hagar, and Yishma'el (*Ishmael*).

The Scenes include Charan (*Haran*), C'na'an (*Canaan*), Sh'chem (*Shechem*), Beit-El (*Bethel*), Ai, Tso'ar (*Zoar*), Plain of the Jordan, S'dom (*Sodom*), 'Amorah (*Gomorrah*), Chevron (*Hebron*), and Dan.

The Main Events include God's promises to Avram, the big trip to a new land, Egyptian detour, Lot's split-off, four kings against five, Yishma'el episode, name changes, and promise of Yitzchak's birth.

his father's house to start a new household in the Promised Land. But first, Avram, along with his household, must be circumcised and await God's timing.

The Trail Ahead ▶

Compass Work

The Path

וַיֹּאמֶר יְהוָֹה אֶל אַבְרָם

לֶךְ לְךָ מֵאַרְצְךָ

וּמִמּוֹלַדְתְּךָ

וּמִבֵּית אָבִיךָ

אֶל הָאָרֶץ אֲשֶׁר אַרְאֶךָּ

—בראשית יב/א

	ךָ	לְ	–	ךְ	לְ
letter:	chaf sofeet	lahmed		chaf sofeet	lahmed
sound:	**CHah**	L'		CH	Leh

go forth, yourself! = LECH L'CHA = לֶךְ לְךָ

The Legend

and said the LORD	*va-yomer Adonai*	וַיֹּאמֶר יְהֹוָה
to Avram	*el-Avram*	אֶל־אַבְרָם
go forth, yourself	*lech l'cha*	לֶךְ־לְךָ
from land-your	*mei-ar'ts'cha*	מֵאַרְצְךָ
& from birthplace-your	*oo-mi-molad't'cha*	וּמִמּוֹלַדְתְּךָ
& from house of father-your	*oo-mi-beit avicha*	וּמִבֵּית אָבִיךָ
to the land	*el-ha-arets*	אֶל־הָאָרֶץ
that I will show you	*asher ar'echa*	אֲשֶׁר אַרְאֶךָּ׃

—Genesis 12:1

Related Words

to go, wander, travel, walk, continue	*halach*	הָלַךְ
to walk, stroll, lead a life	*hit'halech*	הִתְהַלֵּךְ
to walk with God (Gen. 5:22)	*hit'halech et ha-Elohim*	הִתְהַלֵּךְ אֶת הָאֱלֹהִים
law, rule, tradition, Halachah	*halachah*	הֲלָכָה
a law for the future *(Aramaic: for days of Messiah)*	*hilch'ta li-moshicha*	הִלְכְתָא לִמְשִׁחָא
mood, temperament, frame of mind	*halach-nefesh*	הֲלָךְ־נֶפֶשׁ
to follow one's inclination (after his eyes)	*halach acharei einav*	הָלַךְ אַחֲרֵי עֵינָיו
wanderer, wayfarer	*helech*	הֵלֶךְ
walker, hiker	*hal'chan*	הַלְכָן

🚶 Hit the Trail!

Go Start a Household!

> ❝ Now ADONAI said to Avram, "Get yourself out of your country, away from you kinsmen and away from your father's house, and go to the land that I will show you. ❞ —Genesis 12:1

Avram is at Charan, the "crossroads" of his life. Suddenly, the LORD orders him, "Go!"

God orders Avram to walk to an unknown land.

Avram must walk in faith, cutting himself off from his country, his birthplace, and his father's home (Terach is 145; see Gen. 11:26, 32; 12:4). Monumental as it sounds, his departure is immediate and without hesitation.

It does not matter that Avram will find out later where God is sending him (Gen. 12:1). He leaves!

Avram "crosses over" the River F'rat (*Euphrates*). He is a descendant of Ever, an Ivri (*Hebrew*)—one who *crosses over*, whether from the river or, the sages go further, the spiritual, moral divide which isolates the righteous from the rest of the world.

In time, God will reward Avram by covenanting to give back to him land, descendants, a name, a nation, a line of kings, and an everlasting heritage from all the nations of the world.

> **?** Read Lk. 9:59-60. Yeshua calls disciples to follow Him immediately (not even waiting to bury a father!), and to go forth proclaiming knowledge of God. Read Gen 11:32; 12:1-2, 8; 13:4. Explain parallels to Avraham's saving faith.

Not in Egypt

❝ When Avram entered Egypt, the Egyptians did notice that the woman was very beautiful. ❞

—Genesis 12:14

The unknown land of Avram's destination is not Egypt. But famine drives him there, and Avram fears the common folk will kill him to take his beautiful wife!

Avram walks to Egypt, but his stay is temporary.

Avram concocts a plan to fool the Egyptians into bargaining for Sarai, figuring he can move on when interest in her arises. He poses as Sarai's brother, which is half-true [Gen. 12:13; Mid. HaGadol]. The plan goes awry when Par'oh takes Sarai for his harem [Gen. 12:15, 19; Sforno]. Avram is forced to accept gifts from Par'oh, lest he incur hostility.

God protects Sarai and smites Par'oh with a skin affliction (plague!), making cohabitation with Sarai impossible. Par'oh is irate and eventually sends Avram out with an armed escort (Gen. 12:17-20). Avram leaves quickly with cattle, donkeys, slaves (including Hagar), and great wealth. Parallels to the Exodus of the sons of Yisra'el are astonishing!

? Faced with risk of death or telling a half-truth, Avram tells the half-truth. Read Mt. 7:6. Explain whether or not Avram should have told the Egyptians that God is with him and Sarai is his wife.

Not in Jordan

> **"** *Lot, who was traveling with Avram, also had flocks, herds and tents. But the land could not support their living together . . .* **"**
>
> —*Genesis 13:5-6a*

L ot accompanies Avram when he leaves Charan to walk with God. After Egypt, both are enormously wealthy (Gen. 13:2, 5). The herdsmen begin to quarrel, so Avram invites Lot to choose where he wants to live.

Wealth tempts Lot to leave the Promised Land.

Lot follows his materialist instincts and chooses the fertile Jordan plain, which is compared to Gan Eden itself (Gen. 13:10). He splits off and descends. The evil of S'dom comes with Lot's choice (Gen. 13:11, 13). Avram is left above with the high ground.

After Lot's departure, God promises to bless Avram with land and seed, including a permanent holding (Gen. 13:15-16). God instructs Avram to walk the perimeter (Gen. 13:17) of this new possession. This faith walk doubles as an ancient Near East legal ritual for taking final possession [Alter, p. 57n]. Thereafter, Avram moves on to Mamre, where he will buy a cave and seal his faith with a mighty deed (Gen. 13:18).

? *Read Num. 32:1-15. The firstborns R'uven, Gad, and M'nasseh are wealthy with cattle and make the same decision as Lot. Trace out the histories of Lot and these tribes to see how the road to riches leads to war and exile.*

Not in Shin'ar

> **"** When Amrafel was king of Shin'ar, Aryokh king of Elasar, K'dorla'omer king of 'Elam and Tid'al king of Goyim; they made war together . . . **"**
>
> —Genesis 14:1-2a

War breaks out, and Lot is taken east. The international empire consists of four kings from the east, headed by Amrafel, King of Shin'ar.

Avram fights the nations for control of the Land.

The Tower of Bavel originated on the plains of Shin'ar (Gen. 11:2). Now Avram faces the task of rescuing Lot, who has been carried off after the international empire has quashed the rebellion of five locals from the Dead Sea area —including the kings of S'dom and 'Amorah (Gen. 14:8-11).

Avram the Ivri (*Hebrew*, Gen. 14:13) gives chase to the north. He takes a trained force of 318 men born in his household (Gen. 14:14), defeating the kings at Dan in a stealth attack at night! Lot is rescued, along with the spoils of war (Gen. 14:16).

In this way, Avram defeats the nations which control the Land of Promise. He returns triumphant, with the spoils of war.

? *Explain the significance of confronting the nations which unify for war under the king of Shin'ar. Reread Gen. 11:2-4. In what way has God counter-attacked the nations who sought to take heaven by force at the Plains of*

Not in S'dom

❝ The king of S'dom said to Avram, "Give me the people, and keep the goods for yourself." ❞

—Genesis 14:21

Scarcely does Avram return to the Land of Promise when he is met by one of the local leaders, the king of S'dom. The king claims the people whom Avram has recaptured from the international empire. As a part of the deal, the king tells Avram to keep the spoils of war (Gen. 14:21). Avram replies with the first oath ever recorded: "Im michut v'ad s'roch na'al!" (Gen. 14:23)—in other words, "Never! Not a thread nor a sandal thong!" Avram wouldn't take even a bare thread, from the smallest of threads to the largest of threads, lest the king of S'dom claim one day that *he* made Avram rich. Avram is zealous to leave that honor exclusively to God!

Avram refuses all rewards from S'dom.

Next, Avram encounters Melchi-Tsedek, priest of the God Most High and king of Shalem (later, the city becomes Y'rushalayim). To him, Avram tithes. Thereafter, God promises the greatest of rewards (Gen. 15:1-5)!

? *Saving faith rests only in its reward from God. Read Heb. 11:6-9a. Avram walked with God toward Egypt, Jordan, Shin'ar, and S'dom. Review Avram's steps of faith and God's immediate responses in each of these places.*

In the Promised Land

❝ ADONAI said to him, "I am ADONAI, who brought you out from Ur-Kasdim to give you this land as your possession." ❞

—Genesis 15:7

Faith journey leads to the Promised Land: "I am ADONAI, who brought you out . . . " (Gen. 15:7; cf. Ex. 20:2). Avram is brought out of Ur to inherit the Land!

God rewards Avraham in the Promised Land.

God ratifies His promise to give Avram the Land by means of an unconditional covenant. Avram watches as a smoking furnace and fire pass between the pieces of animal which Avram cuts to set up the covenant (Gen. 15:17-21).

Since Avram is not a participant in the covenant ceremony, the covenant is not conditional upon Avram (or his seed) doing anything to merit the Land. God alone promises. The covenant is not based on Avram or his seeds' faith. Rather, it depends solely on God's promise.

Now, God orders Avram to walk before Him and be blameless (Gen. 17:1), the same calling given to Chanoch and Noach. Avram receives a new name with a greater destiny: Avraham, Father of a Mass of Nations (Gen. 17:4-5).

Avraham's actions of tenting the boundaries (Gen. 13:17), cutting the animals (Gen. 15:10, 17-21), and believing God (Gen. 15:6) illustrate the fruits of his faith. Explain how Avraham's faith results in God's promises of reward.

In Covenant Relationship

> 66 "I am establishing my covenant between me and you, . . . generation after generation, as an everlasting covenant, to be God for you and for your descendants after you." 99　　　　—Genesis 17:7

Circumcision is required as the sign of God's covenant with Avraham's physical seed (Gen. 17:10-11). The covenant is a b'rit olam (*everlasting covenant*) between God and Avraham's seed for all time. Mutual covenant responsibilities include God's promise to maintain His part (Gen. 17:4-8) and Avraham's seed's responsibilities to maintain their part (Gen. 17:9-14).

A redemptive picture can be seen of a faithful kingdom living from generation to generation (forever!) in the Land of Promise. Here, God adds the unique statement, "I will be their God" (Gen. 17:7-8).

The covenant between God and His people is personal.

This unique relationship of direct supervision appears throughout the Torah (Ex. 4:5, 6:7; Lev. 11:45; 26:12, 45). Yisra'el is referred to as the only nation directly under God's eyes. A special, personal relationship develops between God, His people, and the Land.

Describe the rewards which God covenants to give Avraham in the Promised Land. Read Genesis 17:14 and Romans 3:1, 4:9-15. Explain the value of circumcision on Avraham's part.

An International Household

" Avraham and Yishma'el his son were circumcised on the same day; and all the men in his household, ... were circumcised with him. "

—Genesis 17:26-27

Instant obedience characterizes Avraham's faith. This obedience is always immediate and exacting. Here, Avraham circumcises every male in his household on that very same day, exactly as God had told him (Gen. 17:23, 27).

The thought staggers the mind that Avraham circumcised hundreds of males "on that very day." His ability to get compliance from all members of his household is mind-boggling! In the days of Yeshua, there were sizable numbers of "God-fearers," who followed Torah—except for circumcision (1 Cor. 7:18-19; Ac. 15:6 ff.).

Yet Avraham circumcised every male, whether Jew or gentile, slave or free (Gen. 17:26-27). A household, composed of men searching for God at the "crossroads" of their faith—an international community—entered into the covenant as a group. What a clear sign that grace cuts across all social lines.

Avraham circumcises men from all nations.

Read Gen. 17:19-21. Explain why Avraham circumcises Yishma'el (who is excluded from the covenant) and the gentiles from his household (who do not require circumcision under the Noachide Laws).

Meander

" As you fan them, the wind will carry them off, and the whirlwind will scatter them. Then you will rejoice in ADONAI, you will glory in the Holy One of Isra'el. "
　　　　　　　　　　　　—Isaiah 41:16

Yisra'el wallows in worm-like despair, cursed with scarce numbers, fear of her enemies, and exile. Yet the LORD tells her not to fear (Is. 41:14). Avram defeated kings with paltry numbers (Gen. 14:1-16); but his seed have not been obedient to the covenant, and the sons of Yisra'el are weak.

The LORD will accomplish His purposes whether Yisra'el obeys or not!

Now God anoints Koresh (*Cyrus*), king of the Persian super-power, to do Israel's work (Is. 41:2-3; 45:1-2). The other nations face Koresh with bigger and stronger idols, but their efforts are hollow (Is. 41:5-7, 11-12).

The LORD has not cast away His covenant people, nor the seed of His friend Avraham (Is. 41:8-9; 2 Chr. 20:7; Jas. 2:23; Jn. 15:15). The LORD will strengthen Yisra'el as a sledge (a flat board used to thresh wheat, with rollers studded with iron spikes). Yisra'el grinds up her enemies and scatters them like chaff to the winds (Is. 41:14-15). Finally, with strength renewed, Yisra'el will rejoice in the LORD!

Reread Is. 40:28-31. Note that the verb actions (Is. 40:31) descend gradually from flying to running to walking. Patience leads to maturity. Are you weary? How can you wait on the Lord and see your strength renewed?

...ings

> **"** ... we have trusted in him who raised Yeshua our Lord from the dead—Yeshua, who was delivered over to death because of our offenses and raised to life in order to make us righteous. **"** —Romans 4:24b-25

Saving faith trusts God as "the one who gives life to the dead and calls nonexistent things into existence" (Ro. 4:17).

God the Father brought Yeshua back to life (Ro. 4:24b-25; 6:4; 8:11; Ac. 3:15; 4:10; Gal. 1:1; Col. 2:12; 1 Thess. 1:10; 1 Pet. 1:21; 1 Cor. 6:14; 2 Cor. 4:14). God the Father also "gave life" to the deadness of Avraham's seed and Sarah's loins for purposes of procreation (Ro. 4:17, which quotes Gen. 17:5 in the Greek LXX; Heb. 11:19).

The circle of life is evident. Yitzchak fathers a line that gives life to Yeshua, and Yeshua offers His life as the human substitute for the ram Avraham offered for Yitzchak.

Saving faith must be walked to be believed.

Saving faith trusts solely in the life-giving power of God the Father to provide for us. God provides for our sins and justifies us by linking Messiah's death to His resurrection. True belief requires us to walk in those beliefs.

? *The second benediction of the Amidah addresses God as the One who "quickens life." Explain whether a lifestyle of saving faith should include fervent prayer for God to "quicken" (breathe life into) hopeless situations in daily life.*

Oasis

Talk Your Walk . . .

Avram responds to the LORD's command, "Go forth, yourself!—Journey! Walk and become a nation!" Immediately, Avram obeys. He saddles up, leaves his aging father at the "crossroads" of Charan, crosses the Euphrates as an Ivri (*Hebrew, crossing over*), and stakes his claim to the promises of land by tenting along the boundary lines.

Famine drives him out. He sojourns to Egypt, where the LORD protects Sarai and inflicts "serious diseases" on Par'oh and his household. Avram leaves Egypt with Sarai (Hagar, too), Lot, and wealth.

Later, the kings from the world empire ally and attack (headed by the king from Shin'ar, where a united mankind built the Tower of Bavel). These kings plunder the land and seize Lot, Avram's nephew. Avram pursues with a small force, conquers them, and retrieves Lot and great booty. He takes nothing for himself, lest the king of S'dom boast that *he* made Avram wealthy.

Avram goes forth, stands up to all nations, and gets God's reward.

The LORD promises Avram the Land, confirming His unconditional covenant with a flaming torch that passes between cut animals. Later, the Lord changes Avram's name to reflect a broader destiny. Avraham and his household enter the covenant through circumcision. They await the time when the LORD will grant him an heir and fulfill the words of His oath.

. . . Walk Your Talk

Have you ever considered that your life is being redeemed right now? Perhaps you believe in eternal security—once saved, always saved. Perhaps you also figure that rewards are unimportant in heaven, because everyone who gets there will be ecstatic. Should you simply rest for now and await the day you meet your Maker?

The author of Hebrews tells us, ". . . it is impossible to be well pleasing to God, because whoever approaches him must trust that he does exist and that he becomes a Rewarder to those who seek him out" (Hebrews 11:6). Faith is central to pleasing God and obtaining lasting rewards. Such rewards are determined by actions

> *To please God,*
> *walk the road of faith.*

in this life. Some-times we must gamble an earthly inheritance for the hope of obtaining a heavenly one. Avram left a comfortable life in Charan to wander as a nomad in the Land, never receiving citizenship there.

Jews today are scattered throughout the world. Some are denied aliyah (*immigration*) as a result of persecution and giants in the land. Still, the greatest rewards are for those seeking God's call. Are *you* going forth? What is God's call on your life? Step by step, the call is the same—Lech l'Cha!

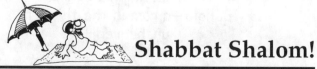

Shabbat Shalom!

וירא

God appeared,
announcing a son!
Avraham fed Him bread.
Sarah laughed over Yitzchak,
just as God said,
until
God asked for Yitzchak's head!

Avraham knew
the request was weird,
until
the angel of God appeared
and cried, "Stop the knife
from cutting his beard!"
Behold—a ram in the thicket,
unsheared!!!

Walk vaYera!
18:1-22:24

וירא

And he appeared

TORAH—Genesis 18:1-22:24
- 1st The LORD Appears!—Genesis 18:1
- 2nd Sarah Fears—Genesis 18:15
- 3rd S'dom Sneers—Genesis 19:1
- 4th The Angel Hears—Genesis 19:21-22a
- 5th Sarah Declares—Genesis 21:5-6a
- 6th Avimelech Swears—Genesis 21:22
- 7th God Dares—Genesis 22:1-2a
- Maftir Nachor Bears—Genesis 22:23-24

HAFTARAH—2 Kings 4:1-37
- Raise Up the Son—2 Kings 4:37

B'RIT CHADASHAH—Luke 1:26-38; 24:36-53
- Raise Up Yeshua—Luke 24:53

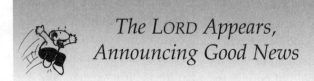

The LORD Appears,
Announcing Good News

Hiker's Log

 ## Looking Back

B'REISHEET (*in the beginning*), God creates paradise perfect, with man as His crown to be fruitful, fill the earth, and rule the world. But man chooses to eat fruit from the Tree of Knowledge of Good and Evil. Disobedience hardens across generations as brother murders brother. Death and exile result. Adam dies, and mankind dies when God judges the world—all except for Noach and his household.

NOACH (*Noah/rest*) is a "righteous-perfect," who walks with God as Chanoch before him. God shows grace to Noach by sparing his household from the waters of judgment. Ten generations later, the LORD commands Avram, LECH L'CHA (*go forth, yourself!*). With his wife and nephew, Avram walks with God, leaving his father's household to start a new household of faith in the Promised Land. God commands Avraham and his house to circumcise themselves. Avraham obeys immediately, along with Yishma'el (soon to become the Arab nations) and an international household. They await the miracle child, heir to the promise of everlasting life.

> **B'REISHEET** *God created man to rule creation.*
> *Man filled his heart with evil, so God raised up* **NOACH** *to rest.*
> *Later, God called to Avram,* **LECH L'CHA!** *Leave everything and start a faith household.*
> *Then,* **VAYERA—** *God Himself appeared!!*

VAYERA YHWH (*and the LORD appeared*) to Avraham, recovering on the third day from circumcision. Avraham, like Noach, finds favor in the eyes of the LORD (Gen. 18:3), Who comes to announce the miracle birth of Yitzchak.

Yitzchak will become the first son in whom hope of eternal life becomes flesh and dwells among us. God not only announces Yitzchak's miraculous entry into life, but also appears again to grant yeshuah (*salvation*) at the akedah (*binding*). His destiny is to laugh—facing death with a glimmer of the resurrection hope of his father who binds him (Heb. 11:11, 19).

Meanwhile, the household of Avraham's brother Nachor expands. Eight sons are born to his wife Milcah (including the father of Rivkah, Yitzchak's future wife). Four more sons are born to R'umah, Nachor's concubine. Nachor's household will exactly mirror Ya'akov's household of twelve sons. The stage is set for households to

In VAYERA . . .

The Key People include 3 angels, Avraham (*Abraham*), Sarah, Lot, Avimelech (*Abimelech*), Yitzchak (*Isaac*), Hagar, Yishma'el (*Ishmael*), and the descendants of Nachor (*Nahor*).

The Scenes include the trees of Mamre in Chevron (*Hebron*), S'dom (*Sodom*) and 'Amorah (*Gomorrah*), Tso'ar (*Zoar*), the Negev, G'rar (*Gerar*), B'er Shava (*Beersheba*), desert of Paran, and Moriah.

The Main Events include the angels' visit, promise of a son, Sarah's laugh, S'dom destroyed, the sister deception part two, Yitzchak born, Hagar and son cast out, treaty, binding of Yitzchak, and God's provision of the ram.

raise tribal chieftains, who can unify to become nations.

The Trail Ahead

Compass Work

The Path

ויָרא אליו יהוה

באלֹנֵי ממרא

והוא ישֵׁב פתח האהל

כחם היום

—בראשית יח/א

	א	רָ	יֶּ	וַ
letter:	alef	reish	yod	vav
sound:	(silent)	**Rah**	Yyei	Vah

and He appeared = VAYERA = ויָרא

The Legend

<u>and appeared</u> to him	*va-yera* elav	וַיֵּרָא אֵלָיו
the LORD	*Adonai*	יְהֹוָה
by the tall trees of Mamre	*b'elonei Mamre*	בְּאֵלֹנֵי מַמְרֵא
and he was sitting	*v'hoo yoshev*	וְהוּא יֹשֵׁב
opening of the tent	*petach-ha-ohel*	פֶּתַח־הָאֹהֶל
in the heat of the day	*k'chom ha-yom*	כְּחֹם הַיּוֹם:

—*Genesis 18:1*

Related Words

to see, look at, behold	*ra-ah*	רָאָה
to witness	*ra'ah b—*	רָאָה בְּ-
to be seen, appear, pretend, seem	*nirah*	נִרְאָה
exhibition, show	*ra'avah*	רַאֲוָה
See you again! (until seeing each other)	*l'hitraot!*	לְהִתְרָאוֹת!
mirror, looking glass	*r'ee*	רְאִי
proof, evidence	*r'ayah*	רְאָיָה
Mt. Moriah	*moriyah, har ha-moriyah*	הַר הַמּוֹרִיָּה

Hit the Trail!

The LORD Appears!

" ADONAI appeared to Avraham by the oaks of Mamre as he sat at the entrance to the tent during the heat of the day. "

—*Genesis 18:1*

Avraham sits outside his tent, sweltering in the heat of the day. It is the third and most painful day since his circumcision.

The LORD appears, in order to confirm His covenant.

In this weakened state, Avraham encounters two angels and the LORD Himself, who appears in order to confirm the covenant of circumcision [Sforno]. Tradition says that Avraham's physical being had become sufficiently purified to be a resting place for God, a "chariot of Divine Presence" [Ber. R. 82:6].

Avraham rises quickly to greet the three visitors. He offers his guests a "morsel" of bread (Gen. 18:5). The morsel grows into a sumptuous meal, including a calf! Commenting on this most excellent display of hospitality, R' Elazar says, "The righteous say [promise] little, do much" [Bav. Metzia 87a]. Sarah kneads the morsel of fine flour (not meal), and Avraham runs to personally choose the calf for the feast [Ramban, Gen. 18:6-7].

Commenting on Avraham's running to select the calf, Stone quotes Talmud to say that "hospitality to wayfarers is greater than receiving the Divine Presence" [Stone, p. 79]. Read Heb. 13:2. What news did God bring? To whom??

Sarah Fears

❝ Sarah denied it, saying, "I didn't either laugh," because she was afraid. He said, "Not so — you did laugh." ❞

—*Genesis 18:15*

Sarah laughs "within herself" when she hears that she and Avraham (a pair of relics!) are to bear a son a year from now. God addresses Avraham; but He is challenging Sarah's unbelief (Gen. 18:12-14), which Sarah denies (Gen. 18:15).

The LORD knows the deepest thoughts of man's hearts.

The Kotzker Rebbe grants that Sarah thinks she has laughed in joy, not in disbelief. However, he concludes that Sarah subconsciously doubts.

Both her post-menopausal reality [Gen. 18:11; B'er Ba Sadeh] and her husband's old age are persuasive.

But God encourages tenderness and mating behavior. He tactfully edits out Sarah's comment (Gen. 18:12) about Avraham's old age, attributing Sarah's words about old age to herself instead (Gen. 18:13). Then He adds words of reassurance by asking, "Is anything too hard for the LORD?" In fact, at the appointed time next year (Gen. 18:14; 17:21), Sarah will indeed bear a son!

? Sarah uses the term 'ednah (cognate with Eden) to contrast her own shriveled skin with the sexual moistness [Alter, p. 79n] necessary to conceive and bear children. Explain why God speaks directly to Sarah's inner thoughts.

S'dom Sneers

❝ The two angels came to S'dom that evening, when Lot was sitting at the gate of S'dom. Lot saw them, got up to greet them and prostrated himself on the ground. ❞   —Genesis 19:1

Hospitality in S'dom is the opposite of life at Avraham's tent! S'dom encourages mistreatment of strangers, fearing that impoverished fortune-seekers would be attracted to its Eden-like fertility [Ramban; Gen. 13:10].

Hospitality is violently discouraged in S'dom.

Lot sits at the gate to the city. Two angels enter as darkness descends. Nights in S'dom are dangerous. Lot extends hospitality to protect the visitors.

Lot's hospitality, however, contrasts with Avraham's. Lot does not follow proper etiquette in offering first to wash his visitors' feet, whereas Avraham does (Gen. 19:2; 18:4). Lot cooks up a "feast" of baked flatbread, whereas Sarah kneads fine flour and Avraham personally selects the fatted calf (Gen. 19:2; 18:6).

But half a loaf is better than no loaf at all—Lot is spared, while S'dom perishes! Aggression against visitors to safeguard the city's prosperity results in divine judgment [Gen. 19:4-5, 9-11; Tos. Sotah 3:11f]. Only Lot will escape.

God appears with two angels in order to prepare Sarah for the confirmation of His covenant and to rescue Lot from destruction at S'dom. Read Heb. 13:2-3, Mt. 25:37-40. How does Lot's hospitality to the angels help save him?

The Angel Hears

> ❝ He replied, "All right, I agree to what you have asked. I won't overthrow the city of which you have spoken. Hurry, and escape to that place . . . ❞
> —Genesis 19:21-22a

Lot is spared—only for the sake of Avraham (Gen. 19:29). Lot's wife is spared for Lot's sake; but she looks back in unconscious disobedience and turns to salt (Gen. 19:26).

Talmud writes that people deserving of punishment cannot look upon the fate of the wicked when they themselves are being spared [Rashi]. Lot loses half of his family, including his wife and his sons-in-law.

The little village, formerly called Bela according to Rashi (Gen. 14:2), is renamed Tso'ar, because Lot calls it "small" (Gen. 19:20, 22). Rashi says the town was saved because its smaller size also accounted for its lesser iniquity.

The rescuing angel grants Lot asylum in a small city.

God poured out His grace upon the town and upon Lot (now an urban dweller) who pleads, "Please let me escape there—isn't it just a small one?—and that way I will stay alive" (Gen. 19:20).

? Compare Avraham's plea for S'dom (Gen. 18:23-32) with Lot's plea for Tso'ar (Gen. 19:17-22). Avraham pleads for divine justice, whereas Lot's plea reflects weakness and convenience. Explain why the angel grants Lot's plea.

Sarah Declares

> ❝ Avraham was one hundred years old when his son Yitz'chak [laughter] was born to him. Sarah said, "God has given me good reason to laugh . . . ❞
> —Genesis 21:5-6a

Triumphant joy replaces denial and unbelief! Sarah declares, "God tz'chok lee (*has brought laughter to me*). All who hear y'tzachak lee (*will laugh*) with me."

Mankind will laugh over the birth of Yitzchak.

Sarah's joy takes place at God's appointed time. True to His promises, God remembers Sarah (Gen. 21:1-2; 18:14). The miracle birth of Yitzchak introduces a new era in the redemption of humankind, because Yitzchak personifies the birth of a son of faith. From the deadened loins of Sarah, only a child of faith could live.

In her joy, Sarah bursts into a three-lined poetic song (Gen. 21:7):

> Who would have predicted to Avraham
> That Sarah would nurse children?
> Yet, I have given him a son in his old age!

Sarah's laughter of disbelief is transformed into the same mirthful wonder that first sprung out from Avraham's heart [Gen. 17:17; Stone, p. 75; Rashi; Onkelos].

Shem gives birth to a firstborn son at the age of 100, exactly one year after exiting the ark (Gen. 11:10).
● *Explain the meaning behind the parallel that connects Shem's son with Avraham's son, ten generations later.*

Avimelech Swears

*" At that time Avimelekh and Pikhol the comman-
der of his army spoke to Avraham. They said, "God
is with you in everything you do. "*

—*Genesis 21:22*

Avimelech and his mil-
itary commander visit
Avraham. This slice
of life that describes
Avraham's relations with his
neighbors will be recreated
again in Yitzchak's life,
and four story segments
in the portion TOL'DOT
will be dedicated to its
resolution (Gen. 26:6, 13,
23-24, 30). Life's choices
are passed across the generations from fathers to sons.

Here, Avimelech and
Phicol see that God favors
Avraham. They fear him
because of this favor and
come to get a treaty [Sforno].

Avimelech asks Avraham to
swear that he will not deal
falsely with him or his son or
his grandson—and here's the
rub—according to the chesed
(*kindness*) I have shown you
(Gen. 21:23).

Avimelech and Avraham covenant at B'er Shava.

Being congenial and affa-
ble, Avraham agrees, saying,"I
swear it" (Gen. 21:24).
Actually, Avimelech's servants
had seized Avraham's well—
so what kindness is Avraham
agreeing to at B'er Shava?

? *Explain whether or not Avraham is wise to go along
with Avimelech's request for a covenant that misrepre-
sents Avimelech's "kindness" to Avraham. Explain
whether Avraham is turning the other cheek to live in peace.*

God Dares

> " *After these things, God tested Avraham. He said to him, "Avraham!" and he answered, "Here I am." He said. "Take your son, your only son, whom you love . . . ''* —Genesis 22:1-2a

Tested! The sages say that Avraham passed ten tests of faith [Av. 5:3], and that the akedah (*binding*) was the last and most severe. Tests bring to light the latent potential in a person, however; and without the test, only God is aware of the person's potential [Ramban].

Avraham unflinchingly obeys in all circumstances.

God tested Avraham, requiring him to leave his land, birthplace, and father's house (Gen. 12:1-3); to give up land that resembled Gan Eden (Gen. 13:5-11); to fight the international empire (Gen. 14); to expel his concubine and son (Gen. 16:5-6); to circumcise himself and his household (Gen. 17:23-27); to relinquish the spoils of war to an evil king (Gen. 14:21-23); and most climactically, to bind his *only* son (Gen. 22:1-3, 9-10)!

In every instance, Avraham hears God's command and ekev (*as a result*) obeys immediately, with a pure heart that pleases God (Gen. 22:16; cf. Dt. 7:12-13).

? Read Gen. 22:16-17. Explain why God responds to Avraham's offer of Yitzchak by swearing an unconditional and irrevocable oath that his offspring will become an eternal nation that can never be destroyed by its enemies.

Nachor Bears

> ❝ B'tu'el fathered Rivkah. These eight Milkah bore to Nachor Avraham's brother. His concubine, . . . Re'umah, bore children also: Tevach, Gacham, Tachash and Ma'akhah. ❞   —Genesis 22:23-24

Nachor gives birth to a twelve-tribe confederation, similar to the sons of Yisra'el. B'tuel, one of eight sons of Nachor by his wife, Milcah (Sarah's sister), fathers Rivkah (Gen. 22:23).

Four names of the secondary sons from Nachor's concubine, R'umah, are also given (Gen. 22:24). Three are personal names [Westermann, vol. 2, p. 368], and the last name describes a region on Mt. Hermon (2 Sam. 10:6-8).

The maftir (*concluding part*) alters the thrust of the portion. Rather than summarizing, it points forward to CHAYEI SARAH (*the life of Sarah*). Rivkah will become Sarah's replacement.

Nachor's confederation-in-embryo fathers Rivkah.

On a grander level, Ya'akov eventually returns to Nachor's house to marry. At that time, the struggle for the pre-eminent confederation will take place. Nachor's son Lavan will try to assimilate Ya'akov before Ya'akov can assimilate Lavan's daughters!

? *Nachor births a 12-tribe confederation. His brother, Avraham, fathers a son and grandson; then the grandson, Ya'akov, fathers a 12-tribe confederation. Why does Avraham have to wait two extra generations for nationhood?*

Meander

Sold into slavery (2 Ki. 4:1-7) or brought back from the dead (2 Ki. 4:8-37)—this week's Haftarah describes children who are redeemed.

In the first episode, a woman beseeches Elisha to save her children from the creditor—Y'horam, son of Ach'av. She cries out that her husband Ovadyahu is dead, and now Y'horam wants to take her children as slaves in the corrupt court of Ach'av and Izevel (*Ahab and Jezebel*). The children will learn corrupt ways, not walking in the God-fearing ways of their father.

Talmud teaches, "He who has raised a son like himself is not regarded as dead" [Baba Kamma 116].

Mothers bear miracle children, saved by faith.

The second episode closely mirrors the Torah portion. Here, the Shunammite woman is granted a miracle son (when she is too old to bear). Later, the son dies unexpectedly. Elisha breathes life into the expired child, who then gets off his death bed—a miracle of life from the dead!

? *Compare and contrast Gen. 18:10, 12-13; 21:2 with 2 Ki. 4:16-17. Explain why the LORD sends an angel or a prophet to foretell the news of a miracle son to be born.*

...ings

❝ And they spent all their time in the Temple courts, praising God. ❞

—Luke 24:53

An angel of the LORD *appeared* in a dream, announcing to Yosef the miracle birth of a son (Mt. 1:20-21; Gen. 17:15-17, 18:10). This news is announced to Miryam as well (Lk. 1:30; cf. Gen. 18:14-15).

> *God appears, then raises up His son—so all men can live through Him.*

As commanded, the couple names the child Yeshua, *"the LORD saves,"* signifying the child's predestined purpose (Mt. 1:21, Lk. 1:31; Gen. 17:21, 21:1-6). His destiny includes restoring David's dynasty and establishing a kingdom without end (Am. 9:11; Lk. 1:32-33; Ac. 15:16-18).

The book of Luke ends as climactically as it begins. Yeshua appears among some followers, telling them not to fear (Lk. 24:36-39). Post-resurrection appearances signal the quickening of "life from the dead" for mankind (1 Cor. 15:45-49). In this way, Yeshua raises up sons like Himself (Is. 53:10)—starting with His disciples who rejoice daily in the Temple and praise God for the gift of eternal life (Lk. 24:53).

? *Read Hebrews 11:17-22. How did Avraham have courage to offer up Yitzchak, even though this action was certain to ruin all that had been promised to him? In what ways can you trust ADONAI with the hopes and dreams of your life?*

Oasis

Talk Your Walk . . .

The LORD appears to Avraham on the third day following his circumcision. Avraham scurries to show hospitality to his visitors, and the LORD announces Sarah will bear a son. Sarah laughs, but then denies laughing to cover up her fear. The LORD laughs last, telling Avraham in advance the name of the child (Gen. 17:19). Sarah finally laughs heartily (Gen. 21:6).

> *The LORD appears at key moments in history to redeem mankind.*

This son is destined to be offered to the LORD as an olah (*ascent offering*), but the LORD will once again appear, to save the child! Avraham's words to his son, YHWH Yireh—*the LORD will see to it,* will be fulfilled through Yeshua nearly 2000 years later.

Like Avraham, Lot also shows hospitality when the angels of the LORD appear. But his household is torn in half at the destruction of S'dom—his wife and two sons-in-law perishing. However, the angel saves a nearby city because of Lot (and Lot is saved because of Avraham's righteousness).

At 100, Avraham fathers his heir (cf. Shem, at 100 fathering his first child, after the flood [Shulman, pp. 21-22]). Avimelech sees "God is with" Avraham, so enters a covenant with him at B'er Shava. Finally, the LORD appears at the akedah (*binding*) and swears to give Avraham an indestructible nation. Meanwhile, Nachor fathers a full-fledged tribal confederacy, complete with twelve sons and a granddaughter, Rivkah.

. . . Walk Your Talk

The scriptures say, "No one has ever seen God" (Jn. 1:18). Yet in this portion, the LORD appears to Avraham. On the one hand, God can be seen when He reveals Himself in some corporeal form (Gen. 33:20); on the other hand, His spiritual essence and glory can never be seen by human eyes (Ex. 33:20). Do you desire to look upon God and live?

Blessed are the pure in heart, for they shall see God (Mt. 5:8). With eyes of faith, one can behold the glory of the LORD. "Seeing" becomes manifest—even as God has

> *Blessed are the pure in heart, for they shall look upon God and live!*

invisibly appeared at the birth of Yitzchak (Gen. 18:14; 21:1-2) and also the birth of Yeshua (Lk. 1:28, 2:9-11).

Always remember that only the pure in heart shall see God. The veil is off for those who look: "So all of us, with faces unveiled, see as in a mirror the glory of the Lord; and we are being changed into his very image, from one degree of glory to the next, by *ADONAI* the Spirit" (2 Cor. 3:18).

Take this minute to reflect upon the way God is transforming you. Imagine a person staring at a pool of water and watching a reflection clarify. The waves subside, and the pool becomes as glass. So it is when you behold the Son of Man and He lives through you.

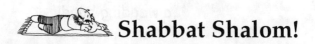 **Shabbat Shalom!**

Now Rivkah continued
חיי שרה
and left her pa
in Charan.
She journeyed in faith
to the promised land,
but couldn't have children
the way she planned.

So Sarah died—
yet Sarah lived.
Her life
continued grand!
In death she embraced
the promised land,
and her son gave Rivkah
a wedding band!

Walk CHAYEI SARAH!
23:1-25:18

Life of Sarah

TORAH—Genesis 23:1-25:18
- 1st Sarah's Sabbatical—Genesis 23:1-2
- 2nd Sarah's Rest in the Land—Genesis 23:17-18a
- 3rd Search for Sarah's Successor—Genesis 24:10
- 4th Appointment with Rivkah—Genesis 24:27
- 5th The Dowry Is Paid—Genesis 24:53
- 6th Avraham's Nations—Genesis 25:1-2
- 7th Yishma'el's Generations—Genesis 25:12
- Maftir Yishma'el's Dominance—Genesis 25:18

HAFTARAH—1 Kings 1:1-31
King David's Successor—1 Kings 1:31

B'RIT CHADASHAH—Matthew 1:1-17
David's Ultimate Successor—Matthew 1:17

*Sarah Lives On
Through Rivkah*

Hiker's Log

 Looking Back

B'Reisheet (*in the beginning*), God creates paradise. He places man in the garden to be fruitful and multiply. Yet man chooses to eat from the tree, increasing chamas (*lawlessness*) upon the face of the earth.

> **B'Reisheet** *God creates,*
> *but man does not rest.*
> **Noach,** *father of mankind,*
> *rests and lives.*
> *Later God calls to Avram,*
> **Lech l'Cha!**
> va**Yera**—*God Himself appears,*
> *announcing Sarah will mother*
> *a miracle son.*
> *The matriarchy lives on—*
> **Chayei Sarah!!**

God sends the waters of judgment from the heavens and the deep to blot out mankind. But first God takes Chanoch, who walked with Him for 365 years. This act of grace enables b'nei adam (*the sons of mankind*) to glimpse the resurrection hope from afar.

Noach (*Noah/rest*) is a "righteous-perfect" like Chanoch, who walks with God. Noach finds chen (*favor*), and by chen (*grace*) the Lord saves him *and his household*. God commands him to build an ark, where he rests for 365 days as the flood waters cleanse the face of the earth. Noach fathers all mankind, as a result of walking with God and resting with Him on the face of the deep (cf. creation's third day when the waters are gathered and dry ground appears).

Ten generations later, the Lord calls, "**Lech l'Cha** (*go forth, yourself!*)." Avram splits off from his idolatrous father, Terach, and starts a new household of faith in the Promised Land. His entire international household enters circumcision and walks in faithful obedience.

In the midst of the painful part of recovery from circumcision on the third day . . . vaYera (*and He appeared*). The LORD Himself announces that Sarah will surely mother Yitzchak, the miracle child and heir to the eternal promise! Years later, the LORD's angel appears, on the third day of the journey to Moriah—this time to spare Yitzchak's very life as his father's faith is tested. (Meanwhile, Avraham's brother fathers a competing household of twelve sons, including Rivkah's father—more about them in the portions ahead!)

The matriarch Sarah dies, but **CHAYEI SARAH** (*life of Sarah*) lives on through the marriage of a new matriarch, Rivkah, to Sarah's son. The LORD plants the family in the Land and

guides the household with the single thought of living out its destiny right there.

The Trail Ahead

Compass Work

The Path

וַיִּהְיוּ חַיֵּי שָׂרָה
מֵאָה שָׁנָה
וְעֶשְׂרִים שָׁנָה
וְשֶׁבַע שָׁנִים
שְׁנֵי חַיֵּי שָׂרָה

—בראשית כג/א

ה	רָ	שָׂ	י	יֵ	חַ
letter: hay	reish	sin	yod	yod	chet
sound: H	**Rah**	Sah	EE	**Yyei**	CHah

life of Sarah = CHAYEI SARAH = חַיֵּי שָׂרָה

The Legend

and there were	*va-yih'yoo*	וַיִּהְיוּ
<u>life of Sarah</u>	*chayei Sarah*	חַיֵּי שָׂרָה
100 year	*meah shanah*	מֵאָה שָׁנָה
and 20 year	*v'esrim shanah*	וְעֶשְׂרִים שָׁנָה
and 7 years	*v'sheva shanim*	וְשֶׁבַע שָׁנִים
years of	*sh'nei*	שְׁנֵי
<u>life of Sarah</u>	*chayei Sarah*	חַיֵּי שָׂרָה:

—*Genesis 23:1*

Related Words

living, alive	*chai*	חַי
fresh water, spring water (living water)	*mayim chayim*	מַיִם חַיִּים
I swear! Upon your life!	*chayecha!*	חַיֶּיךָ!
Cheers! To life!	*l'chayim*	לְחַיִּים
Book of Life	*sefer ha-chayim*	סֵפֶר הַחַיִּים
tree of life	*ets chayim*	עֵץ חַיִּים
prince, princess (ruler, commander)	*sar, sarah*	שַׂר, שָׂרָה
Prince of Peace	*sar shalom*	שַׂר־שָׁלוֹם
God (Prince of princes)	*sar sarim*	שַׂר שָׂרִים

Hit the Trail!

Sarah's Sabbatical

> ❝ Sarah lived to be 127 years old; these were the years of Sarah's life. ❞
>
> —Genesis 23:1-2

How striking to notice a parashah (Torah *portion*) named after a wife! Torah gives no other woman's age—here, Sarah's age is spelled out: 100 years and 20 years [a full life, Gen. R. 58:7] and 7 years (a sabbatical year besides). In this way, Torah distinguishes Sarah as matriarch, the mother of those who believe in God.

But can Sarah rest in the Land? Avraham hastens to bury Sarah, for to inter is praiseworthy [Moed Katan 22a]. Avraham, as an onen (*mourner*), negotiates to purchase the grave site.

But here's the irony— Avraham is an alien and a resident foreigner among the Hittites. Strangers are not permitted burial rights!

Sarah dies without a grave site in the Land.

Avraham approaches the sons of Chet (Hittites, Gen. 10:15). Efron heads the council at Kiryat Arba, for adjacent the field is a double cave—the Machpelah!

? *Torah couples Rivkah's birth (Gen. 22:23) to Sarah's death (Gen. 23:1-2). The righteous leaves only after another righteous is born to take his/her place [Sforno]. Explain how Rivkah can take the place of Sarah, Avraham's wife.*

Sarah's Rest in the Land

> **❝** *Thus the field of 'Efron in Makhpelah, which is by Mamre—the field, its cave and all the trees in and around it—were deeded to Avraham as his possession . . .* **❞**
> —Genesis 23:17-18a

Avraham pays the steep price of 400 shekels for Sarah's grave site—well beyond its worth. King David will pay far less for the Temple site (2 Sam. 24:24)!

> *In death, Sarah receives a legal foothold in the Land.*

The negotiation is tricky. Avraham prevails upon the council to let him pay full price and bury his wife (Gen. 23:8-9). He is told, "Bury your dead" (Gen. 23:11). No price is given! A second time, Avraham insists on paying full price (Gen. 23:13). Only then does Efron quote an outrageous price, asking, "What is 400 shekels between you and me?"

Avraham just happens to be carrying that much around! He immediately weighs out the silver as legal tender (Gen. 23:16), validates the deed as a permanent possession (Gen. 23:18), and confirms the full agreement of the community for its use as a burial place (Gen. 23:18, 20).

? *Read Gen. 23:17. The Midrash translates the verb "vayakom" with its literal meaning "to arise" or become "elevated." In what sense does the transfer of ownership from a Hittite to Avraham "elevate" the land? Explain.*

Search for Sarah's Successor

> **"** *Then the servant took ten of his master's camels and all kinds of gifts from his master, got up and went to Aram-Naharayim, to Nachor's city.* **"**
> —*Genesis 24:10*

Ten camel loads of gifts form part of the mohar (*bridal dowry*) for Yitzchak's wife (cf. Gen. 34:12). Avraham turns from Sarah's burial to the pressing need of a wife for Yitzchak. Only through a son can the family line continue.

Avraham sends off his trusted servant (Eli'ezer) with an oath and a promise of divine guidance, but no guarantee of success (Gen. 24:7-8). Upon arrival, the trusted servant prays to the LORD (Gen. 24:12). He requests a sign to convince the girl's family to release the girl for a distant marriage. Immediately, the divine appointment commences (Gen. 24:15).

The servant with the dowry asks God for a sign.

Stunned, Eli'ezer watches as Rivkah compassionately offers him water and then races to draw water for all his thirsty camels! She keeps running, until she has poured 140 gallons of water into the trough [*Family Chumash*, p. 123; Gen. 24:19-20].

Compare Genesis 24:20 with Genesis 18:7. To what extent does Rivkah's spirit of hospitality rival that of Avraham? Explain why Eli'ezer lavishes gifts of gold before he even knows who the girl is (Gen. 24:22-23).

Appointment with Rivkah

❝ *Then he said, "Blessed be* ADONAI, *God of my master Avraham, who has not abandoned his faithful love for my master; because* ADONAI *has guided me . . ."* ❞
　　　　　　　　　　　　　　　　　　—Genesis 24:27

Eli'ezer responds to Rivkah's gracious hospitality by bowing in prayer and praising the LORD! In selfless abandonment, Eli'ezer thanks God for His steadfast guidance and direction.

Upon seeing the sign, Eli'ezer turns his attention to the LORD and addresses Him as the God of his master, Avraham. God is not a local deity, "for He has led me straight to my master's relatives." Above all, he thanks the LORD God for His chesed ve'emet (*covenant loyalty and truthfulness*) to Avraham.

Chesed ve'emet underlies God's plan for redeeming mankind (Gen. 24:49; Ex. 34:6), regardless of man's unworthiness.

> *Eli'ezer praises the* LORD *for kindness to Avraham.*

God's chesed ve'emet move Lavan and B'tuel, too. Lavan responds, ". . . take her and go . . . as ADONAI has said" (Gen. 24:51; note 24:48-52). Lavan will later reverse his words, but this will provide Rivkah an opportunity to exercise faith!

? *The spiritual man is in constant communion with God through prayer. Read 1 Thess. 5:17, Lk. 18:1-7. Explain* • *how God deals with the prayers of the faithful. Do you pray frequently enough? selflessly enough? fervently enough?*

The Dowry Is Paid

> ❝ *Then the servant brought out silver and gold jewelry, together with clothing, and gave them to Rivkah. He also gave valuable gifts to her brother and mother.* ❞
> —Genesis 24:53

Bridal moneys are paid out once an agreement is reached. The procedures here follow a "sistership document," a kind of Hurrian contract used in Charan [Speiser, pp. 184-185].

Rivkah is released to journey to the Promised Land.

Key provisions include the brother (Lavan) acting to negotiate in place of the father (B'tuel), gifts being given to the mother and brother, a dowry for the bride, and the need for informed bridal consent. Thus, the gifts given at the well (Gen. 24:22) do not count as part of the dowry.

There is a question concerning whether Lavan wishes to break the engagement and take the gifts. Lavan reverses his earlier response and requests a delay for "days or ten" [Stone, p.118; Ket. 57b]. "Days" can mean years (Lev. 25:29). The parties defer to Rivkah, who states emphatically, "Elech! (*I will go!*)" (Gen. 24:58, cf. Gen. 12:1, 4), ending the struggle over both bridal consent and timing.

? Rivkah follows the footsteps of Sarah to the Land, and even marries Yitzchak in Sarah's tent (Gen. 24:67).
● Explain how Rivkah carries on the life of Sarah, beginning childless in Ur and ending a nomad buried at Machpelah.

Avraham's Nations

> " *Avraham took another wife, whose name was K'turah. She bore him Zimran, Yokshan, Medan, Midyan, Yishbak; and Shuach.* "
>
> —*Genesis 25:1-2*

Nations descend from Avraham in fulfillment of covenant promises (Gen. 12:2a, 17:4-6). Through K'turah, Avraham fathers sons whose names are identified with a number of Arab tribes.

Avraham gives gifts to his sons of concubines (Hagar and K'turah) while he is living and then sends these sons out from the land of C'na'an (Gen. 16:2, 25:6). Yitzchak, however, son of Avraham's wife Sarah, receives the testamentary gift reserved for heir of the everlasting covenant (Gen. 25:5).

Thus, "giving while you're living" is the rule observed for sons born by concubines (cf. Code of Hammurabi), whereas the heir receives the remainder of the estate, as a heritage to be passed on to the tol'dot (*generations*) to come.

Sons by concubines do not receive a land heritage.

In the book of SH'MOT (*names/Exodus*), this patriarchal heritage will grow from a family of tribes to a nation. Yisra'el, as its father, will form the nation's character, name, and destiny.

? *These sons of K'turah include the Midyanim, who were active in the international spice trade in the Arabian desert. Read 1 Ki. 10:1-10, Is. 60:6. How does Midyan contribute to the future glory of Y'rushalayim?*

Yishma'el's Generations

> ❝ *Here is the genealogy of Yishma'el, Avraham's son, whom Hagar the Egyptian woman bore to Avraham.* ❞
>
> —*Genesis 25:12*

Blessed are the seed of the righteous! In deference to Avraham, God blesses Yishma'el with twelve tribes (a national confederation), great fruitfulness, and long life (Gen. 25:12-18).

Yishma'el receives blessing for honoring his father.

The Yishma'elim live in open cities, the circular camps of nomads (Lev. 25:31). These cities are unwalled, reflecting the promises of peace and security. Other encampments, headed by tribal chieftains, reflect organization that supports the promised blessing of a national confederation.

Yishma'el's wanderings range from Sinai (Abdeel) to Babylonia (Kedar, Massa, N'vayot). The Itureans (sons of Jeter) are mentioned in the New Covenant (Gen. 25:15; Lk. 3:1). Tribes from the sons of N'vayot (Gen. 25:13) and Kedar (Is. 42:11) participate in the glory of Y'rushalayim in the millennial days (Is. 60:7). Esav, mourning his loss of eternal promises arising from intermarriage, marries Machalat, N'vayot's sister (Gen. 28:19).

? *Read Gen. 16:2-5. Avram listens to Sarai and conceives Yishma'el. After Sarai exiles Hagar, the angel addresses her as a maidservant and orders her to submit to her mistress (Gen. 16:7-9). Explain the angel's apparent partisanship.*

Yishma'el's Dominance

> **"** *Yishma'el's sons lived between Havilah and Shur, near Egypt as you go toward Ashur; he settled near all his kinsmen.* **"**
>
> —Genesis 25:18

Yishma'el's sons become twelve leaders; and the tribal groups grow into a great nation, as promised to Avraham (Gen. 17:20). The fulfillment of this promise sets the stage for TOL'DOT, the next portion which deals with the *generations* of Yitzchak, heir to the covenant promise.

In Yishma'el, it becomes apparent that the promise of fruitfulness also leads to a need to expand into the lands of brothers dwelling nearby.

Yishma'el spreads out into Havilah, where his eastern boundary is carved out in the region of northern Arabia (Gen. 2:11; 10:7); in Asshur, the northern boundary of his lands carves out the region of Sinai (others say Syria).

Yishma'el dominates all concubines' sons.

In this way, population growth and land conflict escalate alongside one another. Yishma'el's offspring are counted for abundance, but his hand is against everyone, and over all his brothers does he dwell (Gen. 16:10-11).

? *The life of Sarah can be measured by the legacy she leaves. She is mother of all believers. Her son, her only one, is heir over all of Avraham's other sons. Explain God's chesed ve'emet to Sarah.*

Meander

❝ Bat-Sheva bowed with her face to the ground, prostrating herself to the king, and said, "Let my lord King David live forever." ❞

—1 Kings 1:31

David and Avraham both face problems of successorship in their old age. Avraham's successorship goes smoothly, because he obtains the oath of his trusted senior servant, Eli'ezer. The LORD directs Eli'ezer's path, and thus, assures the marriage and continuation of the house of Avraham and Sarah.

Here, King David confronts a crisis. His fourth-born son, Adoniyahu, has declared himself to be the next king (1 Ki. 1:5) at a solemn gathering (1 Ki. 1:9) which has excluded Sh'lomo, the true heir to the throne (1 Ki. 1:10). Natan visits Bat-Sheva to warn her that her life and her son's life are in danger (1 Ki. 1:11-12).

Orderly succession of David's dynasty is assured by David's oath.

Only David can declare his successor (1 Ki. 1:20), and he comforts his wife with an oath that Sh'lomo will succeed him (1 Ki. 1:30). The oath, now in the LORD's hands, so assures the outcome that the Haftarah ends before it is reported.

? Compare Gen. 3:16 with 1 Tim. 2:11, 15. Now search for similarities between 1 Ki. 1:31 and 1 Pet. 3:6. Both Sarah and Bat-Sheva treat their husbands with extraordinary respect. In what way does this untangle a Gan Eden pattern?

...ings

> **" Thus there were fourteen generations from Avraham to David, fourteen generations from David to the Babylonian exile, and fourteen generations . . . to the Messiah. "** —Matthew 1:17

David's dynasty of kings and Avraham's heir to the promises of the household converge in Yeshua haMashiach.

> **Born of a woman, Yeshua is Avraham's heir and David's son.**

The sacred text introduces Yeshua as the son of David, the son of Avraham (Mt. 1:1). His heritage passes through Yitzchak, Ya'akov, Y'hudah among the brothers, and Peretz among the twins (Mt. 1:2-3). It passes through David and Sh'lomo among the kings (Mt. 1:6). Four gentile women appear as matriarchs. The text climaxes with Miryam, mother of Yeshua (Mt. 1:16). Sarah's household has its ultimate fulfillment in Yeshua, King at the end of a dynasty of kings!

The genealogy is segmented into three periods of 14 generations each— Avraham to David, David to the exile, and the exile to the birth of Messiah (Mt. 1:17). In gematria (see glossary), the Hebrew letters in David's name sum to 14. Messiah Himself is the last "David" to redeem David's fallen dynasty from the curse of exile.

> **?** Read Amos 9:11-12 and Acts 15:16-18. The LORD Himself promises to return and restore. Compare Sarah's experience of barrenness to the virgin Miryam's experience when the LORD appears, proclaiming the miracle birth of a son.

Oasis

Talk Your Walk . . .

CHAYEI SARAH (*life of Sarah*) starts with Sarah's death. Sarah is the only woman in Torah whose age is given: 100 + 20 + 7 years. One hundred twenty years denotes a full life; perhaps the additional seven years point to a sabbatical rest. In death, Sarah rests in the land she couldn't own in life.

Avraham pays what is required to own the royal burial plot. In his negotiations, the head of the Hittite council which approves the purchase asks seven years' wages of a common laborer to bury Sarah in Chevron!

Sarah's life continues through Rivkah, the bride of Yitzchak.

Thereafter, Avraham searches for a successor matriarch to mother his grandchildren through Yitzchak. He requires an oath from his trusted steward, Eli'ezer, whom he sends out to his brother's household in Charan on a mission to find a Shemite wife for his son.

The LORD guides Eli'ezer to Rivkah, a hospitable woman. She literally follows Sarah's footsteps to the Promised Land—right to Sarah's very tent, where she marries Yitzchak and continues the line. Meanwhile, Yishma'el (Sarah's son by her concubine) begets a twelve-tribe confederation which dominates all surrounding tribes.

. . . Walk Your Talk

The path of progressive redemption calls for a faith journey. Without knowing it, you may find yourself living out a destiny that enables man to "walk with" God. Neil Armstrong lighted on the moon, saying "That's one small step for man, one giant leap for mankind!" Such is the call of our faith journey. In like manner, Rivkah elects to walk the same 300-mile trek which Sarah walked when she "crossed over" to start a new, international household of faith in the Promised Land. Rivkah continues *the life of Sarah* when she enters into the same faith and same dream —leaving the Aramean house of Nachor in Charan to marry Yitzchak in Sarah's tent.

You are called to continue the same faith journey. But you must trust God with the key decisions of your life. This is more than theory—you must be willing to take reproof and correction from those with whom you pray.

Are you willing to let Yeshua live through you?

Yeshua lives through those who continue His life.

Read Matthew 6:33—Seek God's kingdom first, and then all these things will be added. Looking at your actions, in what ways can you honestly say that you are "walking with" God and that Yeshua is living His life through you?

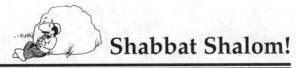

Shabbat Shalom!

תולדת, תולדת,
have a son—
Yitzchak, Yitzchak,
the only one!
Pick Esav or Ya'akov,
twins for fun.
God chose Ya'akov
as the תולדת son.

Esav wanted
to have the blessing,
but Ya'akov
stole it instead.
Esav said,
"I'll kill him dead!"
So Ya'akov
upped and fled!

Walk TOL'DOT!
25:19-28:9

Generations

TORAH—Genesis 25:19-28:9

HAFTARAH—Malachi 1:1-2:7

B'RIT CHADASHAH—Romans 9:1-13

*The Coming Generations
of Yitzchak*

Hiker's Log

 ## Looking Back

B'REISHEET (*in the begin-ning*), God creates par-adise. Man disobeys God's command and eats from the forbidden tree. God responds to the ever-increas-ing evil of chamas (*lawlessness*) by blotting out mankind.

> **B'REISHEET** *God creates.*
> *Only* **NOACH** *rests.*
> *God calls to Avram,* **LECH L'CHA.**
> *Suddenly,* **VAYERA!**
> *God announces a son.*
> **CHAYEI SARAH** *lives on*
> *in the faith household*
> *through the coming generations—*
> **TOL'DOT.** *Twins, take one!*

Only **NOACH** (*Noah/rest*) is spared. Like Chanoch, Noach walks with God in trust and obedience. When his house-hold is redeemed from judg-ment, Noach fathers all mankind. The Noach-Shem connection begins a line of Shemite priests.

Ten generations later, the LORD calls, "**LECH L'CHA** (*go forth, yourself!*)." Avram walks a faith journey to the Land of Promise. His entire interna-tional household gets circum-cised while awaiting an heir.

The third day following circumcision, **VAYERA** (*and He appeared*)! The LORD Himself announces that Sarah will mother Yitzchak, heir to the promise that the LORD will redeem all nations of mankind. The angel of the LORD appears again 38 years later at Moriah— this time to save Yitzchak's life and promise Avraham an inde-structible nation. Meanwhile, Avraham's brother fathers a parallel family of twelve sons in Charan.

CHAYEI SARAH (*the life of Sarah*) continues through death, as the first land holding is purchased to provide a permanent resting place for her. Rivkah is called to make the same 300-mile faith journey from Charan (*the crossroads*) to the Promised Land, where she continues Sarah's life by marrying Yitzchak in Sarah's tent!

Thus, the household continues with new TOL'DOT (*generations*). Twin nations emerge, battling even before their birth. Ya'akov is dispatched to Charan not only to escape his brother's wrath, but also to find a wife from Nachor's family (a competing nation-in-embryo). However, first Yitzchak must obey the LORD, face famine in the Promised Land, claim his father's wells, and deal with Avimelech—all this to ground Avraham's covenant in the Land of eternal rest.

In TOL'DOT . . .

The Key People include Ya'akov, Yitzchak (*Isaac*), Rivkah (*Rebecca*), Esav (*Esau*), Avimelech (*Abimelech*) king of the Philistines, daughters of Chet (*Het*), Lavan (*Laban*), and more wives for Esav.

The Scenes include G'rar (*Gerar*), B'er Shava (*Beersheba*), Yitzchak's 3 wells, Shiv'ah (*Shibah/seven*), and Paddan Aram.

The Main Events include the Lord speaking to Rivkah, birth of twin nations, the birthright traded for stew, famine, prosperity in G'rar, Yitzchak's blessing for Ya'akov when tricked by hairy skin, the blessing reaffirmed, Ya'akov sent to Lavan to get a wife, and Yitzchak bestowing Avrahamic blessing on Ya'akov —the next generation to receive divine favor.

The Trail Ahead ➡

Compass Work

The Path

ואלה תולדת
יצחק בן אברהם
אברהם הוליד
את יצחק

‏—בראשית כה/יט

letter:	ת	ד	לְ	ו	ת
	tav	dalet	lahmed	vav	tav
sound:	T	**Doh**	L'	OH	Tt

generations = Tol'dot = תולדת

The Legend

and these (are)	*v'eleh*	וְאֵלֶּה
<u>generations</u> (of) Isaac	*tol'dot* Yitz*chak*	תּוֹלְדֹת יִצְחָק
son of Abraham	*ben-Avraham*	בֶּן־אַבְרָהָם
Abraham	*Avraham*	אַבְרָהָם
gave birth to	*holeed*	הוֹלִיד
— Isaac	*et-Yitzchak*	אֶת־יִצְחָק׃

—Genesis 25:19

Related Words

derivative	*tolad*	תּוֹלָד
result, consequence, offspring, corollary	*toladah*	תּוֹלָדָה
historian, chronicler	*toladan*	תּוֹלְדָן
history, chronology, generations	*toladot*	תּוֹלָדוֹת
biography, life story, vitae	*tol'dot chayim*	תּוֹלְדוֹת חַיִּים
to bear children, beget, bring forth	*yalad*	יָלַד
boy, girl	*yeled, yaldah*	יֶלֶד, יַלְדָּה
childhood	*yaldoot*	יַלְדוּת

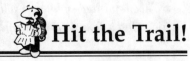 **Hit the Trail!**

These, the Generations

> **"** Here is the history of Yitz'chak, Avraham's son. Avraham fathered Yitz'chak. **"**
>
> —*Genesis 25:19*

TOL'DOT is translated as *offspring* [Rashi] or *life story* [Sforno]. Here, the term tol'dot describes the eternal seed and land inheritance Yitzchak passes to his heir.

> *Yitzchak is the only heir to pass on the covenant.*

Avraham's son Yishma'el, half-brother of Yitzchak, is omitted. Both Yishma'el's line (Gen. 25:12-18) and Kayin's line (Gen. 4:17-24) precede the line of the father and son chosen to pass on the promise of redemption for all mankind (Gen. 5:1 ff.; 25:19).

As Avraham's "only" son of faith, Yitzchak lives out Hevel's life as a second-born "slain-in-faith." Recall that Shet is "appointed" to replace the murdered Hevel (Gen. 4:25). Now, Avraham passes life on to his son apart from murder.

TOL'DOT Yitzchak (*Isaac's life story*) will mirror his father's. Like Avraham, Yitzchak will face problems of famine, problems over a beautiful but barren wife, problems over wells, problems over prosperity; and like Avraham before him, Yitzchak will pass on God's covenant to the next generation.

? Read Mt. 23:35-36; 24:2. *Murder is part of the curse of the covenant. Explain how the murder of Hevel is part of the accumulated judgment which falls on the generation in which God's Temple is destroyed stone by stone.*

Yitzchak Digs In

Famine strikes Yitzchak's line as in Avraham's day (Gen. 26:1). Perhaps to preempt the birth of another Yishma'el, VAYERA elav YHWH (*and the LORD appeared to him*)—ordering Yitzchak not to follow his father's footsteps to Egypt. Twice God promises him "all these lands" (Gen. 26:3-5), based on the oath He swore to Avraham (Gen. 22:16-18).

Yitzchak remains in G'rar. The famine hits hard [Riva, in Tos. haShalem]. Yitzchak must be encamped near Avraham's wells, for he weathers the famine, sows, and reaps one-hundred-fold in the land (Gen. 26:12).

Yitzchak obeys and reaps prosperity in the Land.

Not only has Yitzchak avoided a second wife, but he reaps prosperity in the land. This harvest in the midst of famine lays the foundation for the unifying of his grandsons, by means of the harvest given Yosef in Egypt.

Read Gen. 28:15, 31:3, and 46:4. What do these verses have in common with Gen. 26:3? Explain how God's presence guarantees protection and success (cf. Gen. 39:2). How does this relate to Yeshua's promise in Mt. 28:20?

Blessed, but Envied

❝ The man became rich and prospered more and more, until he had become very wealthy indeed. ❞

—Genesis 26:13

Tension, jealousy, and animosity from others always seem to accompany God's blessings of multiplication, prosperity, and affluence in the patriarchs' lives (Gen. 13:2-7; 30:25-43; 30:1; 37:11; cf. Ex. 1:7, 20-22).

Yitzchak prospers in the midst of persecution.

Envied due to his prosperity, Yitzchak is expelled from the foreign land of Avimelech (Gen. 26:15-16). Never mind that expelling Yitzchak violates a covenant with Avraham, concerning his wells and his seed [Gen. 21:27; Mid. haGadol].

To keep the peace, Yitzchak meekly moves on. At G'rar, he digs new wells, different from the ones belonging to his father which the P'lishtim stopped up (Gen. 26:15). He names his wells Esek (*contention*), Sitnah (*enmity*), and R'chovot (*spaciousness*). The last well taps into an underground source of "living waters" [Gen. 26:19; Ramban].

? *Yisra'el's enemies say, "Yes, you dug the well. The <u>hole</u> belongs to you, but the water is ours" [Hirsch in Stone, p. 133]. Read Gen. 26:12; Mk. 10:29-30. In what way does Yeshua link God's blessing of prosperity to persecution, too?*

Leave Well Enough Alone!

*" From there Yitz'chak went up to Be'er-Sheva.
ADONAI appeared to him that same night and said,
"I am the God of Avraham your father . . ." "*
                                   —Genesis 26:23-24a

Yitzchak moves on to B'er Shava. His life events clearly following those of his father (Gen. 21:22-34): the same setting, B'er Shava; the same negotiators, Avimelech and Phicol; the same motivations, "God is with you"; the same end, a non-aggression pact.

> *Yitzchak forgives, though Avimelech does not repent.*

God has already spoken to Yitzchak to comfort him over the loss of his wells. God tells him not to fear. Yitzchak's property will not be diminished from strife.

Avimelech has noticed that God is with Yitzchak. According to Targ. Yonatan, after Yitzchak's departure, Avimelech's wells dry up and his fruit trees fail to produce fruit. Avimelech seeks a treaty, possibly to annul the effects of cursing on his wells and trees: "Let there be an oath between us . . . that you will not harm us, just as we have not caused you offense but have done you nothing but good" (Gen. 26:29). Yitzchak remains easygoing and agrees to the oath.

> **?** *Read Gen. 26:27: "Once burned, shame on you. Twice burned, shame on me!" Read Mt. 18:21-22; Lk. 17:3-4. If someone steals your valuable wells, is it better to seek repentance or move on? Is Yitzchak a pushover? Explain.*

B'er Shiv'ah—Well Seven

> 66 *Yitz'chak prepared a banquet for them, and they ate and drank. The next morning, they got up early and swore to each other. Then . . . they left him peacefully.* 99
> —Genesis 26:30-31

Yitzchak consummates mutual acceptance of the covenant treaty by preparing a feast. Here, the meal precedes the swearing of

Yitzchak and Avimelech swear to live and let live.

the oath (Gen. 26:30-31).

Immediately thereafter, "that very day," Yitzchak's servants confirm digging well number seven (Gen. 26:32). God rewards Yitzchak with discovery of water in B'er Shiv'ah (*well seven*).

Some Talmudic sources say that the plain sense of the word *seven* is not meant; rather, *oath* is the intended meaning [Tan. Yashan; vaYetse 9]. Against this, Ibn Ezra sees a tie to the seven ewes Avraham gave Avimelech to commemorate the first treaty (Gen. 21:28-31). Swearing an oath confirms Yitzchak's claim on the land.

Thus, a key event in the life of Yitzchak takes place. The oath now transfers across tol'dot (*generations*), with reference to a pre-existing oath [Onkelos, Mizrachi]. Well Seven is B'er Shava, the Well of Swearing.

> ? • *Note the movement of the text from Gen. 26:24 to Gen. 26:25 to Gen. 26:28. Read Prov. 16:7. In what way does Yitzchak make his enemies to be at peace with him? Explain the role God plays in blessing Yitzchak's choices.*

The Stolen Blessing

> **❝** *So may God give you dew from heaven, the richness of the earth, and grain and wine in abundance. May peoples serve you and nations bow down to you . . .* **❞**
> —*Genesis 27:28-29a*

Yitzchak starts by granting Ya'akov agricultural blessings: dew of the heavens so important for crop yields, fatness of the earth, abundant grain, and wine. He concludes with blessings of political supremacy: authority over peoples, over nations, and over his mother's sons (Gen. 27:28-29). These blessings parallel blessings granted Avraham (Gen. 12:2, 14:19-20).

Ya'akov exits, and Esav returns with game from the hunt. Yitzchak trembles violently, realizing that Ya'akov has usurped the blessing he had planned to give Esav.

Ya'akov obtains blessings Yitzchak reserved for Esav.

That Yitzchak is deceived does not mean he can or will change his decision. In grief, he tells Esav, "Look, I have made him your lord, I have given him all his kinsmen as servants, and I have given him grain and wine to sustain him. What else is there that I can do for you, my son?" (Gen. 27:37).

?• *Compare the blessings of land and seed (Gen. 28:3-4) with those reserved for Esav (Gen. 27:28-29). The latter bestow material blessings of abundance, power, dominion, and pre-eminence. Are these stolen blessings? Explain.*

One Son Marries

❝ *So Yitz'chak sent Ya'akov away; and he went to Paddan-Aram, to Lavan, son of B'tu'el the Arami, the brother of Rivkah, Ya'akov's and 'Esav's mother.* **❞**

—Genesis 28:5

Only two verses mark off this section, the shortest in the Torah! Yitzchak sends Ya'akov away, both to flee Esav's wrath and to marry a relative in the home of his mother's brother.

Ya'akov commanded to marry a non-Canaanite.

Ironies abound. Rivkah, hoping to save her son from Esav's wrath, never sees Ya'akov again. She dies before he returns from a lengthy absence.

Then Esav, following Lemech the Kayinite's path toward extinction, commits bigamy and assimilates (Gen. 36:2; cf. Gen. 4:19). For the first time, Esav seems to realize that his marriages have caused grief to his parents (Gen. 28:8-9). Yet Esav neither repents of his marriages, nor divorces his wives! He does, however, feel sorrow over the loss of the TOL'DOT blessing which Ya'akov receives to sustain him on the road to Paddan-aram (Gen. 28:3, 4, 6).

? *Intermarriage is a major issue among Jewish people. Jews should not marry idolaters. Read 1 Cor. 9:20.*
● *Generally speaking, should parents encourage believing Jewish children to marry believing Jewish children, or not?*

One Son Assimilates

❝ 'Esav also saw that the Kena'ani women did not please Yitz'chak his father. So 'Esav went to Yishma'el and took, in addition to the wives he already had, Machalat . . . ❞   —Genesis 28:8-9

Esav now realizes that he has forfeited the eternal promises of land and seed—the TOL'DOT blessing—as a result of assimilation.

Esav assimilates, falling short of spiritual blessing.

It is ironic that Esav, now married 23 years, has been so out of touch with his parents' anguish over his assimilation. Esav never seemed to grasp that Rivkah followed Sarah's footsteps for hundreds of miles to journey from the "other side" and marry in the Land of Promise.

Esav's attempted solution is to marry Yishma'el's daughter, Machalat. The older brother, N'vayot, gives her in marriage, perhaps because Yishma'el has died [Rashi].

This ploy to set aside the question of assimilation falls short, however. Still marginalized by his Hittite wives, Esav merits neither the blessing nor the birthright, a heritage reserved for the everlasting TOL'DOT Yitzchak (*generations of Isaac*). However, the part of Esav's line through Yishma'el continues as Edom, thereby averting the annihilation suffered by Kayin and C'na'an.

Why couldn't Esav's line through Machalat, daughter of Yishma'el, daughter of Avraham, preserve the sacred line of Avraham, Yitzchak, and Esav? Explain whether or not children of Machalat should be excluded from the covenant.

Meander

Priests are charged with the calling to revere the LORD's name (Mal. 2:1-2). But the kohanim (*priests*) have despised Him (Mal. 1:6), offering blemished sacrifices (Mal. 1:7; Lev. 22:18-20).

Priests are called to keep the Levitical covenant.

So repugnant is this to the LORD that He will curse the priestly privilege of channeling blessings of life and peace to the people (Mal. 2:2, 5). The curse will affect "the seed," the coming generations of Levi (Mal. 2:3). In fact, the covenant with Levi may not pass from this generation.

High standards are required of priests (Mal. 2:4). Ideal priests walk in awe of the LORD (Mal. 2:5-6). They are the teachers and guardians of moral life, warned to live uprightly as mal'achim (*messengers*) to pull up the people (Mal. 2:7). Omitted from the Haftarah reading are the next two verses, which judge this generation and threaten to halt the passing of the covenant to the sons of Levi (Mal. 2:8-9; Mal. 1:2-3).

Read Mal. 1:2-4. ADONAI says that Esav's nation will be called "The Land of Wickedness" and "The People with Whom the LORD Is Forever Angry." Can Esav's seed rebuild the ruins of their nation? Explain why or why not.

...ings

❝ . . . it was said to her, "The older will serve the younger." This accords with where it is written, "Ya'akov I loved, but 'Esav I rejected." ❞

—Romans 9:12-13

Again, the LORD uses a man's name for his posterity. TOL'DOT describes *"generations that follow."* In the Torah, Yitzchak's generations are Ya'akov (who will live through his sons). In the Haftarah, Levi's covenant describes the priests to come.

> ## Divine calling sets the stage for promises made to future generations.

Here, Rav Sha'ul reviews that his countrymen according to the flesh birthed Messiah according to the flesh (Ro. 9:3, 5). Not all of Avraham's children, however, will inherit the seed of promise (Ro. 9:7-8).

Rather, Ya'akov is selected—not on the basis of works (for he had not yet done good or evil), but solely on the basis of calling (Ro. 9:11). God's choice is made while the twins are in the womb! Prior to birth, God calls Ya'akov.

The principle that the elder shall serve the younger (Ro. 9:12) sets the stage for the LORD's plan of redemption. Yitzchak will pass on his heritage to Yisra'el, father of a nation. Yisra'elim are beneficiaries of this everlasting heritage!

? *Read Ro. 4:17; 8:29-30. What does it mean to be called, made right, and glorified according to divine purposes?*
● *Does despising your birthright matter? Explain the role of "works" in your calling. Are "works" unimportant?*

Oasis

Talk Your Walk . . .

The TOL'DOT (*generations*) from Yitzchak through his twin sons, Esav and Ya'akov, grow into separate nations. Even before they are born, the LORD prophesies that the older will serve the younger. Esav, strong and violent, emerges first; but true to the LORD's word, his nation will serve the sons of Ya'akov.

The LORD commands Yitzchak to remain in the Land despite a famine. When Avraham faced famine, he went to Egypt where Sarah acquired Hagar, an Egyptian maid who birthed Yishma'el. Yitzchak avoids this tangent. The LORD prospers him, enabling him to reap a hundred-fold for his efforts. Life isn't struggle-free, however. Avimelech forces Yitzchak from his father's wells and even the wells his servants dig. Yitzchak moves to B'er Shava. Avimelech follows and, seeing Yitzchak's wealth, covenants to live in peace.

> The LORD orders Yitzchak to redeem the mistakes of his father.

To his parents' dismay, Esav feasts with Hittites and intermarries. Yitzchak still wants to bless Esav, but Rivkah conspires with Ya'akov to snatch the blessing. Aggrieved, Esav purposes to repeat the sin of Kayin (and kill his brother). Ya'akov flees to Charan, to escape his brother's wrath and marry a Shemite from Nachor's family. Esav eventually mourns his intermarriages and marries a daughter of Yishma'el. Too little, too late—the inheritance passes to Ya'akov.

. . . Walk Your Talk

Have you ever counted the cost of marrying an unbeliever? Sarah, Rivkah, and later Leah, Rachel, and their maidservants journeyed over 300 miles in faith to enter the Promised Land.

A heritage spans generations and requires a faith journey. The same trials that your parents faced are presented to you! It is your destiny to face these trials and stand on the shoulders of those who have gone before you.

Like Avraham, Yitzchak was married to a beautiful wife when facing Avimelech. Fortunately, the LORD had protected Sarah, and His protection made life easier for Yitzchak! Yitzchak also faced famine in the land, but the LORD blessed him and helped him reap a hundred-fold. The wealth convinced Avimelech that the LORD was with Yitzchak, resulting in a covenant at B'er Shava

> *We stand on our parents' shoulders, reaching high for God.*

(*the well of swearing*). Thus, Yitzchak made progress in redeeming the Land. In what way can you say that you are living a redemptive life? Are you making life simpler for the coming generation?

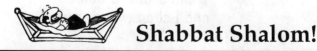

Shabbat Shalom!

וַיֵּצֵא Ya'akov—
he went out from the land.
Find a wife! Make sons!
It's time to expand!
A ladder of angels,
and God's helping hand
to keep Ya'akov safe—
God did what He planned.

So Jake married twice!!
Then God was praised—
Y'hudah was born!
Many sons were raised!!!!!!!!!!!!
Protected by God,
even cattle who grazed,
all returned home
and Laban was dazed.

Walk vaYetse!
28:10-32:2(3 תנ״ך)

וַיֵּצֵא

And he went out

Torah—Genesis 28:10-32:2(3 תנ״ך)
- 1st Exit, Ya'akov!—Genesis 28:10
- 2nd To Charan—Genesis 29:1
- 3rd Love—Genesis 29:18
- 4th Barrenness—Genesis 30:14
- 5th Wealth—Genesis 30:28
- 6th Another Fast Get-Away—Genesis 31:17-18
- 7th Caught!—Genesis 31:43a
- Maftir Return, Ya'akov!—Genesis 32:1-2(2-3 תנ״ך)

Haftarah—Hosea 11:7-14:9(10 תנ״ך)
- Walk or Stumble—Hosea 14:9(10 תנ״ך)

B'rit Chadashah—John 1:19-51
- Climb and Ascend!—John 1:51

Ya'akov Exits,
but God Promises a Comeback

Hiker's Log

 ## Looking Back

B'REISHEET (*in the beginning*), God creates paradise. Man disobeys, choosing a path of exile, destruction, and death. These are the consequences of introducing knowledge of evil.

> **B'REISHEET** *God creates.*
> *Only* **NOACH** *rests.*
> *God calls to Avram,* **LECH L'CHA**.
> **VAYERA!** *God announces a son.*
> **CHAYEI SARAH** *lives on*
> *through new* **TOL'DOT**
> *in the faith household.*
> *But when the family struggles,*
> *Ya'akov exits—***VAYETSE**.

NOACH (*Noah/rest*) rests in the ark and finds favor in the eyes of God, while corporate mankind dies in the flood. Thereafter, mankind multiplies, but tries to unify to take heaven by force. The LORD introduces language to frustrate man's efforts and spread him out in disunited nations.

Then the LORD calls to Avram, **LECH L'CHA** (*go forth, yourself*)! Avram begins a faith journey to the Promised Land and circumcises his entire international household.

The third day following circumcision, **VAYERA** (*and He appeared*)! The LORD announces that barren Sarah will mother Avraham's heir. Later, when Avraham offers up Yitzchak to the LORD in faith, the LORD's angel swears that ekev asher shamata b'koli (*as a result of your heel-like obedience to my voice*), Avraham will father an indestructible nation.

CHAYEI SARAH (*the life of Sarah*) continues the life of a saved household: Sarah lives on through Rivkah's matriarchy, Avraham lives through Yitzchak's patriarchy, and the saved household lives on.

The promise is extended across **TOL'DOT** (*generations*),

as Yitzchak secures his father's wells in the land. On another level, twin nations in Rivkah's womb fight for firstborn rights. Ya'akov emerges second, clutching at his brother's heel. He manipulates to obtain both the birthright and the blessing, but he is forced to flee his brother's wrath.

VAYETSE Ya'akov (*and Jacob went out*) to Charan, his ancestral home at the crossroads. Along the way at Beit-El, the LORD promises a safe journey. He exits to avoid the household assimilation facing Esav in C'na'an. At Charan, he will meet and wish to marry Rachel. But his scheming uncle, Lavan, has other ideas. Ya'akov will be delayed from returning for twenty years and will nearly assimilate into Nachor's heathen nation in exile. In the end, angels at Machanayim will welcome Ya'akov back home to the Land.

In VAYETSE . . .

The Key People include Ya'akov (*Jacob*), Rachel, Lavan (*Laban*), Leah, maids, and sons.

The Scenes include B'er Shava (*Beersheba*), Beit-El/Luz (*Bethel*), Charan (*Haran*), Gal'ed (*Galeed*), and Machanayim (*Mahanaim*)

The Main Events include Ya'akov's escape, dream of angels ascending and descending, God's promise of family and land, Ya'akov's response to build altar and tithe, 20 years of work (7 for Leah, 7 for Rachel, 6 for livestock), 11 sons born, livestock increase, dream warning Ya'akov to return home, a fast getaway while Lavan chases, the family gods stolen by Rachel, the Lavan/Ya'akov covenant at Gal'ed, and angels greeting Ya'akov at Machanayim.

The Trail Ahead

Compass Work

The Path

ויצא יעקב
מבאר שבע
וילך חרנה

—בראשית כח/י

letter:	א	צֵ	יֵ	וַ
	alef	tsadee	yod	vav
sound:	(silent)	**TSei**	Yyei	Vah

and he went out = VAYETSE = וַיֵּצֵא

The Legend

<u>and went out</u>	*va-yetse*	וַיֵּצֵא
Jacob	*Ya'akov*	יַעֲקֹב
from Beersheba	*mi-B'er Shava*	מִבְּאֵר שָׁבַע
and walked	*va-yelech*	וַיֵּלֶךְ
Charan-toward	*Charanah*	חָרָנָה:

—*Genesis 28:10*

Related Words

to go out, leave, expire, be exempt, defecate	*yatsa*	יָצָא
exit, departure, emigration, death, expense	*y'tsiah*	יְצִיאָה
the Exodus from Egypt	*y'tsiat Mitsrayim*	יְצִיאַת מִצְרַיִם
to die, breathe his last (went out his spirit)	*yats'ah rucho*	יָצְאָה רוּחוֹ
to become famous (went out his name)	*yatsa sh'mo*	יָצָא שְׁמוֹ
to be published (went out to light)	*yatsa la-or*	יָצָא לָאוֹר
extraordinary (went out from the rule)	*yatsa min ha-c'lal*	יָצָא מִן הַכְּלָל
blessing for bread coming forth from ground	*ha-motsi*	הַמּוֹצִיא
for from Zion comes forth the Torah	*ki mi-Tsiyon tetse Torah*	כִּי מִצִּיּוֹן תֵּצֵא תוֹרָה

Hit the Trail!

Exit, Ya'akov!

> **" Ya'akov went out from Be'er-Sheva and traveled toward Haran. "**
>
> —*Genesis 28:10*

Ya'akov exits to flee from Esav and find a wife (matriarch) to continue the TOL'DOT (*generations*) of his fathers.

Ya'akov exits the Land and is promised a safe return.

How ironic that Yitzchak (who could never leave the land!) sends his son out of the Land. The shvi'i (*seventh*) section will highlight this irony.

Ya'akov encounters an unexpected theophany before departing the Land of Promise. At a place he will name Beit-El (*House of God*), Ya'akov dreams of a vast ramp with terraced landings [Alter, p. 149]. Hamilton [p. 239] likens the ramp to a stairway connecting the Land of Promise and heaven (cf. Gen. 11:4).

Standing over him, the LORD bestows the eternal covenant promises given the patriarchs: seed (before he has children) and land (safe passage and safe return, even before he has exited). In fact, the LORD promises to be with Ya'akov and never forsake him in exile (Gen. 28:15).

? God's promised Presence is critical to Ya'akov's survival in exile. Read Gen. 28:20-22. Ya'akov vows that upon return, he will tithe in the Lord's house. Is Ya'akov accepting the LORD as God now, or after his trip? Explain.

To Charan

> " Continuing his journey, Ya'akov came to the land of the people of the east. "
>
> —Genesis 29:1

Eastward and northward goes Ya'akov, to the ancestral home. Torah tells us that the clans of Shem and Ever spread out to the east (Gen. 10:30). One must cross over the river to reach Charan. Thus, Ever's clan becomes known as those who have come to C'na'an "from the other side" of the River.

Ya'akov journeys east, to the ancestral home.

Others, without exception, wander "to the east" under a cloud of exile (Gen. 3:24), judgment (Gen. 4:16), rebel-lion (Gen. 11:2), materialistic desire (Gen. 13:11), or disin-heritance (Gen. 25:6).

In contrast to these others who wander to the east, Ya'akov enters exile accompa-nied by the LORD. Behold, YHWH nitsav (*the LORD stands*) over Ya'akov at Beit-El, promising His abiding Presence (Gen. 28:13-15).

Ya'akov vows to enter into covenant with ADONAI upon safe return. Later, the sons of Yisra'el journey east and NITSAVIM (*are standing*), ready to enter the Land God promised the fathers (Dt. 29:10-15).

? Ya'akov (2108-2255) could have heard about humankind's first ancestral home, in Gan Eden, third-hand from Adam (0-930), who told Lemech (874-1651), who told Shem (1558-2158). Discuss whether Ya'akov heard Shem's story.

Love

❝ *Ya'akov had fallen in love with Rachel and said, "I will work for you seven years in exchange for Rachel your younger daughter."* ❞

—Genesis 29:18

In lieu of a bridal price, Ya'akov offers a seven-year labor of love for Rachel, the girl of his dreams. The language follows that of a legalistic betrothal; and the specific language spells out the younger daughter, as well as the term of indentured service (Gen. 29:15, 18).

Ya'akov works for fourteen years to marry two wives.

Ya'akov wants the agreement to be a matter of public knowledge so that Lavan, the brother, cannot deny or twist the terms of the agreement [Or haChaim].

No matter! Ya'akov, the "heel grabber," reaps the very deceit that he sowed by posing as Esav (Gen. 27:35; 29:25). Lavan puts Leah, the older daughter, under a veil and marries her off first, saying, "In our place, that isn't how it's done, to give the younger daughter before the firstborn" (Gen. 29:26).

Perhaps the underlying irony hushes Ya'akov, but he agrees to wait a week and then work another seven years for Rachel.

God sees that Leah is unloved (Gen 29:31). Leah bears three children, hoping that each one will win her husband's love. Then she bears Y'hudah. Read Gen. 29:32-35. To whom does Leah give credit for Y'hudah? Explain.

Barrenness

" During the wheat harvest season Re'uven went and found mandrakes . . . Rachel said to Le'ah, "Please give me some of your son's mandrakes [so that I can be fertile]." "
>
> —Genesis 30:14

Mandrakes ripen in the harvest months of April and May (Nisan, Iyar, and Sivan). These stalkless plants send up large leaves which fan out from the root, at ground level.

Barrenness creates tension among Ya'akov's wives.

The violet flowers are followed by a yellowish, tomato-like fruit, still called "love apples" today. The fruit emits a distinct scent, and the Hebrew name for it, dudaim, derives from the word dod—meaning *lover* (Song of Songs, 7:13-14).

The three- or four-year-old R'uven scoops up some of these ancient aphrodisiacs and comes home. Both wives are struggling with barrenness: Rachel for years, and Leah after "leaving off" following the birth of Y'hudah. Rachel pleads for the aphrodisiacs. Leah chides Rachel for coming between her and her husband (Gen. 30:15). Sforno sees Leah as chiding Rachel for marrying Ya'akov at all (cf. Lev. 18:18).

? Both wives give their concubines to bear children (Gen. 30:3-8, 9-13). Read Ps. 127:3. In previous generations, concubines' sons were excluded from the inheritance; yet here, concubines' sons become heirs. Explain.

Wealth

❝ "... Name your wages," he said; "I will pay them." ❞

—*Genesis 30:28*

Name your wage! Lavan knows he has prospered on account of God's blessing on Ya'akov: "A blessing follows immediately upon the entertaining of a scholar" [Ber. 42a]. Lavan fears that Ya'akov's departure could reverse his fortunes. He has already lengthened Ya'akov's stay an additional seven years. A new round of bargaining is needed.

Ya'akov argues that he has worked hard, and Lavan's livestock "have increased substantially" as a result of the LORD's blessing on everything that Ya'akov undertakes (Gen. 30:29-30).

Lavan and Ya'akov cut a new deal.

Lavan again asks Ya'akov to name his wages (v. 31). Ya'akov proposes a deal based on caring for sheep and goats, giving Lavan the lavan (*white*) ones and giving Ya'akov the non-white (supplanted) ones. Ya'akov's livestock increases substantially over the next six years, while Lavan's attitude sours.

? *Read Gen. 31:1-3. Explain why the LORD directs Ya'akov to return to the ancestral home of his fathers. Relate your answer to God's covenant promise (Gen. 28:15).*

Another Fast Get-Away

> " *Then Ya'akov got up, put his sons and wives on the camels, and carried off all his livestock, along with all the riches . . . to go to Yitz'chak his father in the land of Kena'an.* "
> —Genesis 31:17-18

Go out!—Ya'akov tells his wives that God, who spoke to him in a dream at Beit-El, has commanded him, Tse' (*Go out*)! The command echoes VAYETSE (*and he went out*), the name of the portion.

Ya'akov's wives do not need convincing, so Ya'akov packs up the camels and exits without telling Lavan.

> *Ya'akov listens to God, and he makes a fast exit.*

The Hebrew text describes Ya'akov's departure (Gen. 31:17), saying literally that he took et-banav v'et-nasav (*his sons and his wives*). Jewish commentators mention that Esav packs up et-nasav v'et-banav (*his wives and his sons*), noting wryly that Esav put personal lust ahead of his family (Gen. 36:6), whereas Ya'akov assigns primary responsibility to fathering a nation—hence his household [Gur Aryeh].

Ya'akov is heading for a crunch. Twenty-two years before, he exited, escaping the wrath of Esav. Now, he sneaks out on Lavan, kindling wrath once again.

? Notice that Ya'akov builds a household complete with livestock in a foreign land. In what ways does the destiny of this patriarch depict the building of Yisra'el in Egypt? Explain God's advance promise in Gen. 15:13-16, 18.

Caught!

> ❝ Lavan answered Ya'akov, "The daughters are mine, the children are mine, the flocks are mine, and everything you see is mine! ❞
>
> —Genesis 31:43a

Ya'akov flees Paddan-aram and "crosses over" the river (Gen. 31:21). On the third day, Lavan learns of Ya'akov's departure, gives chase for a week, and closes in at Gal'ed.

Lavan attempts to keep Ya'akov's house in Aram.

God warns Lavan, that night in a dream, not to harm Ya'akov (Gen. 31:24). The next day, Lavan accuses Ya'akov of sneaking out and stealing. Ya'akov responds, angrily unloading twenty years of pent-up frustration! Livestock that were attacked, he paid for (though shepherds are exempt!); he served 14 years for wives; and without God's help, he'd be empty-handed right now!!

Lavan appeals to the Assyrian law of erebu—echoing Gen. 2:24, a man joins his wife's family and household! Leah's and Rachel's children are Nachor's great-grandson's grandsons—if Ya'akov goes out, his wives, children, and cattle must stay in Aram [Plaut, p. 212n., on Gen 31:43].

? Read Gen. 31:43-47. Ya'akov and Lavan conclude a treaty with a covenant meal, setting boundaries at the "Witness Pile." (Gal'ed in Hebrew, and Yegar-sahadutha in Aramaic). Do these boundaries separate nations? Explain.

Return, Ya'akov!

> " Ya'akov went on his way, and the angels of God met him. When Ya'akov saw them, he said, "This is God's camp," and called that place Machanayim [two camps]. "
> —Genesis 32:1-2(2-3 תַנ"ך)

Twin camps of angels are sighted by Ya'akov, both when he exits the Land and when he returns to the Land. One camp keeps watch over the Land, and the second camp provides safe escort for those who go out [Rashi; note that the Hebrew ending "-ayim" on the word "camp" indicates a *pair* of camps].

The angels ascend and descend (Gen. 28:12). In explaining the order, Rashi notes that the first company of angels ascends to heaven on the ramp or stairway, and then the other company of angels descends to escort the travellers.

Ya'akov exits and enters with an angelic escort.

Then on the return, the reverse process occurs. Angels in the Land await the return and then come out to meet Ya'akov. It is not the troops of Esav or Lavan who are coming to attack; rather, it is the camps of angels sent to protect God's people from their enemies [Targ. Yonatan].

? *In the next portion, Ya'akov divides his family and flocks into two camps. Do Machanayim and Ya'akov's camps have anything in common? Read Mt. 6:10 from the Lord's prayer. Explain how deeds on earth affect heaven.*

 **Meander**

> **" Let the wise understand these things, and let the discerning know them. For the ways of ADONAI are straight, And the righteous walk in them, but in them sinners stumble. "** —Hosea 14:9 (10 תנ״ך)

The LORD's judgment mingled with love and mercy is summarized in the above verse concluding the Haftarah. Efrayim has turned against the LORD (Hos. 13:16/14:1 תנ״ך) and will die.

> ### Repent from idolatry and rise from the dead.

The people wanted kings; in wrath, the LORD gave and took them away (Hos. 13:11). Yisra'el's first king, the Efrayimite leader Yarav'am (*Jeroboam*), set up gold calves (at Beit-El, of all places!) to keep the people from journeying to the Temple.

No Yisra'eli king ever repudiated Yarav'am's idolatrous ways (1 Ki. 14:16; 15:30; 16:2, 13, 19, 26, 31; 22:52; 2 Ki. 3:3; 10:31; 13:2, 11; 14:24; 15:9, 18, 24, 28; 17:22; summarized in 2 Ki. 17: 21-23).

Efrayim is accountable; and after 19 idolatrous kings, Efrayim dies to patriarchal leadership (Hos. 13:1). Note also that the idolater Terach, a 19th generation son of Adam, dies cut off from his son Avraham, the patriarch of nations (Gen. 11:32). Even so, the LORD still promises to restore Yisra'el (Hos. 14:1, 5-9/2, 6-10 תנ״ך).

? *Read Hos. 13:15. Assyria plunders Efrayim, leading the people into permanent exile. Efrayim falls (Hos. 13:16/ 14:1 תנ״ך) and Yisra'el stumbles (Hos. 14:1/2 תנ״ך). Has Yisra'el stumbled so as to fall? Explain Rom. 11:11.*

...ings

> **Then he said to him, "Yes indeed! I tell you that you will see heaven opened and the angels of God going up and down on the Son of Man!"**
>
> —John 1:51

Yeshua meets "an Israelite indeed," a descendant of Ya'akov who is without guile [Tenney, p. 41]. Referring to Ya'akov's experience at Beit-El (Gen. 28:10-19), Yeshua tells N'tan'el he will receive revelation even greater than Ya'akov's. Then Yeshua reveals Himself as the ladder, the contact point between heaven and earth!

Yeshua tells N'tan'el how heaven and earth connect.

Yeshua says the angels ascend and descend "on the Son of Man" (Jn. 1:51). The Midrash (*exposition*) interprets Gen. 28:13, "ADONAI nitsav alav (*the* LORD *was standing upon him/it*)," to mean *on Ya'akov*, not *on the ladder* [Mid. R. 69:3]. Yeshua's application fits snugly into N'tan'el's understandings; thus N'tan'el becomes Yeshua's disciple.

Ya'akov watched, as the heavens were opened. Now Yeshua, the Son of Man in heaven and on earth (Jn. 3:13), descends to give life to the world (Jn. 6:27, 53). When His work is accomplished, He ascends to glory (Jn. 6:62) and takes His seat at the right hand of God (Mt. 26:64).

? *Yeshua tells N'tan'el that he will "see heaven open," just as Ya'akov saw heaven open at Beit-El. What does it mean for heaven to open? Is heaven ever closed? What difference would N'tan'el's experience make in your life?*

Oasis

Talk Your Walk . . .

VAYETSE/*And he went out* in a speedy exit from the Promised Land. The "Heel-grabber/ Supplanter" Ya'akov is forced to flee his twin brother's wrath as a result of conspiring to steal the blessing. He begins a lengthy journey to the house of Nachor in Charan, encountering angels at Beit-El.

Exiled from his home, Ya'akov becomes a "wandering Aramean" like his grandfather. Ya'akov's journey to Aram contrasts sharply with Yitzchak's wait in the land for the arrival of his bride, Rivkah. Ya'akov gets hung up in Charan for twenty years! He must endure intricate maneuvering by his uncle Lavan and competition among his wives (for children). In fact, he nearly assimilates—except the LORD orders him home.

> *Ya'akov exits, but the LORD promises a safe comeback.*

Ya'akov sneaks out with his wives and wealth, but Lavan pursues and plans to seize everything. According to the Assyrian law of erebu, wives and property belong to the maternal household, not to the husband [Gordon, p. 249 ff.]. The LORD confronts Lavan in a dream the night before he catches Ya'akov and warns him to say nothing (evil) to Ya'akov. In the end, Lavan and Ya'akov covenant (one in Aramaic, the other in Hebrew) to respect each other's boundaries. Then Ya'akov goes on to Machanayim (*Twin Camps*) where again he encounters angels and sees new boundaries separating heaven and earth.

. . . Walk Your Talk

Like Ya'akov, we too are called to "walk with" God; and by faith, we can walk our way to heaven. Chanoch "walked with" God. Noach "walked with" God. Avraham and Yitzchak "walked with" God (Gen. 48:15), and Ya'akov passed this blessing on to the sons whom he adopted—both Efrayim and M'nasseh. Even Eli'ezer the C'na'ani "walked with" God (Gen. 24:40). It makes no difference whether one is from Yisra'el or from the nations—even from the accursed nation. Man always has been called to "walk with" God.

In Gan Eden, Adam and Chavah heard the sound (or voice) of the LORD "walking with" Himself in the cool of the day (Gen. 3:8). This kind of intimate walk is intrinsic to the very nature of God! Knowledge of God causes us to hide ourselves from intimacy when God asks, "Where are you?" (Gen. 3:9).

> *At Machanayim, heaven meets earth in the Promised Land.*

Our Creator still awaits our return to Gan Eden. He purposes to redeem all the earth. He calls us to "walk with" Him until we, along with Ya'akov our father, come home to Machanayim. To what extent are you listening to the voice of the One Who calls?

Shabbat Shalom!

וישלח sent Ya'akov
gifts to his brother,
asking forgiveness
for deceit with his mother.
He feared for his life
and both wives, one another,
scared that big brother
his family would smother.

But Esav received him
without being mad,
though Ya'akov didn't trust
that Esav was glad.
He gave back the blessing
without being sad,
but refused Esav's escort,
fearing Esav was bad!

Walk VAYISHLACH!
32:3(4ּתנ״ך)-36:43

And he sent

TORAH—Genesis 32:3(4ּתנ)-36:43
- 1st Sendoff to Se'ir—Genesis 32:3(4ּתנ)
- 2nd Send Off the Gifts—Genesis 32:13(14ּתנ״ך)
- 3rd Mugged—Genesis 32:30(31ּתנ״ך)
- 4th Paying Tribute—Genesis 33:6
- 5th Shame!—Genesis 34:1-2
- 6th The Land Heritage—Genesis 35:12
- 7th Se'ir's Land First—Genesis 36:20-21
- Maftir Edom's Land Next—Genesis 36:43

HAFTARAH—Obadiah 1:1-21
Yisra'el Will Prevail—Obadiah 1:21

B'RIT CHADASHAH—Hebrews 11:11-20
Yisra'el's Land at Last—Hebrews 11:20

Ya'akov Sends All to Come Home

Hiker's Log

 Looking Back

B'REISHEET (*in the beginning*), God creates a perfect paradise. Man is created in the image of God, to co-partner the task of ordering and ruling over creation. But man chooses to go his separate way, introducing the knowledge of good and evil into the order of creation. As a result, mankind will incur judgment at the flood for allowing chamas (*lawlessness*) to rule over creation.

Only **NOACH** (*Noah/rest*) finds favor in the eyes of God. Unlike Adam, he cooperates with God, obeys by building an ark, and rests in the waters of the flood with his wife, three sons, and their wives. Corporate mankind dies in the flood, but Noach weathers judgment and fathers all the sons to follow. Ten more generations pass. The nations go their own way again, build the Tower at Bavel, and attempt to take heaven by force. In response, God introduces languages. Mankind's unity in rebellion fragments, and mankind scatters throughout the world as the "seventy" separate nations of the world.

> B'REISHEET *God creates,*
> *but only* NOACH *rests.*
> *God calls to Avram,* LECH L'CHA.
> *Then* VAYERA*! God announces*
> *Sarah will be matriarch.*
> CHAYEI SARAH *lives on*
> *through Rivkah*
> *and* TOL'DOT *Yitzchak.*
> *When Ya'akov is chosen,*
> *twin brothers fight*
> *and Ya'akov flees—*VAYETSE.
> *He shall return, though,*
> *sending gifts—*VAYISHLACH
> *and yes, the stolen blessing, too.*

Then God calls to Avram (the *exalted father*), LECH L'CHA (*go forth, yourself!*). Avram begins a faith journey on the road to an identity change. God soon renames him Avraham (*father of a multitude of nations*). To ensure the building of the nation, vaYERA YHWH (*the LORD appeared*) with a birth announcement.

CHAYEI SARAH (*the life of Sarah*) continues across the TOL'DOT (*generations—both life events and offspring*). Twin nations are born to the successor household, and vaYETSE Ya'akov (*out went Jacob*) to escape his brother's wrath. But 22 years later or so, come back he must. That's when vaYISHLACH Ya'akov (*Jacob sent out*) messengers, to read his brother's intentions so he could obey God and return to the Land. Ya'akov learns that Esav is coming to "greet" him with a raiding party of 400 men!

In VAYISHLACH . . .

The Key People include Ya'akov (*Jacob*) renamed Yisra'el (*Israel*), Esav (*Esau*), messengers, sons of Chamor (*Hamor*), Dinah, Sh'chem (*Shechem*), D'vorah (*Deborah*), Rachel, Binyamin (*Benjamin*), 12 sons, and Yitzchak (*Isaac*).

The Scenes include Se'ir (*Seir*), Edom, Yabok (*the Jabbok*), P'ni'el (*Peniel*), Sukkot (*Succoth*), Sh'chem (*Shechem*), Luz—later renamed Beit-El (*Bethel*), Efrat (*Ephrath*), and Mamre.

The Main Events include sending tribute; all-night wrestling, Ya'akov renamed Yisra'el; Esav encounter; Dinah shamed, town circumcised, then killed; house purified and altar built at Beit-El, eternal promises of children and land repeated; death of Rachel on road, Binyamin's birth; visit to Yitzchak, death, burial by both sons; Esav's generations, and Esav's move to Edom.

Ya'akov prepares furiously all night long.

The Trail Ahead

Compass Work

The Path

וַיִּשְׁלַח יַעֲקֹב מַלְאָכִים
לְפָנָיו אֶל עֵשָׂו אָחִיו
אַרְצָה שֵׂעִיר שְׂדֵה אֱדוֹם

—בראשית לב/ד

letter:	chet	lahmed	shin	yod	vav
	ח	לַ	שְׁ	יֲ	וַ
sound:	CH	**Lah**	SH	Yyee	Vah

and he sent = VAYISHLACH = וַיִּשְׁלַח

The Legend

<u>and sent</u> Jacob	<u>va-yish</u>lach Ya'akov	וַיִּשְׁלַח יַעֲקֹב
messengers	mal'achim	מַלְאָכִים
before him	l'fanav	לְפָנָיו
to Esau brother-his	el-Esav acheev	אֶל־עֵשָׂו אָחִיו
land-toward Seir	artsa Se'ir	אַרְצָה שֵׂעִיר
field (of) Edom	s'deh Edom	שְׂדֵה אֱדוֹם׃

—Genesis 32:3(4ת‏נ״‏ך)

Related Words

delegate, envoy, messenger, emissary, agent	shaliach	שָׁלִיחַ
treats sent on Purim	shalach manot	שָׁלַח מָנוֹת
missile, weapon, javelin; sprout, shoot, plant	shehlach	שֶׁלַח
dismissed, driven out, abandoned, divorced	shulach	שֻׁלַּח
Let my people go! (Ex. 7:16)	shalach et ami	שַׁלַּח אֶת עַמִּי
scapegoat	sa'ir ha-mishta-le-ach	שֵׂעִיר הַמִּשְׁתַּלֵּחַ
by proxy (on the hand of a messenger)	al-y'dei shaliach	עַל־יְדֵי שָׁלִיחַ
relay race (running messengers)	me-rots sh'lichim	מֵרוֹץ שְׁלִיחִים
mission, errand; message	sh'lichoot	שְׁלִיחוּת

Hit the Trail!

Sendoff to Se'ir

> **❝** *Ya 'akov sent messengers ahead of him to 'Esav his brother toward the land of Se'ir, the country of Edom . . .* **❞**
>
> —*Genesis 32:3 (4 תֹנִ"ך)*

Mal'achim (*angels*) greet Ya'akov at Machanayim (*Twin Camps*). Now Ya'akov sends off his own mal'achim (*messengers*) to greet Esav at his field at Edom in Se'ir.

Ya'akov prepares to meet Esav, his brother, in Se'ir.

Oddly, Ya'akov's messengers return, unharmed and with no word, except a report that Esav is coming to meet him with a 400-man party. Ya'akov has no way to know whether Esav is advancing for a military confrontation (1 Ki. 20:27; 2 Ki. 23:29; cf. Num. 20:20) or coming to greet him in a friendly manner (as Rivkah greeted Yitzchak, her husband-to-be in Gen. 24:65; note also 2 Ki. 8:8-9; 9:18).

Ya'akov is seriously stressed! He forms his own "twin camps," with wives in one and concubines in another, and he prays earnestly (Gen. 32:7-12/8-13 תֹנִ"ך). Next, he will prepare a minchah (*tribute*) to soften his brother's wrath over the stolen blessing and birthright (Gen. 27:32-36).

? Read Genesis 32:6(7 תֹנִ"ך). Explain why Esav would let Ya'akov's messengers return unharmed and without a reply. What is Esav's intent in coming to greet Ya'akov with a 400-man raiding party?

Send Off the Gifts

❝ He stayed there that night; then he chose from among his possessions the following as a present for 'Esav his brother: . . . ❞

—*Genesis 32:13* (14־ךְ ")

Ya'akov repents stealing Esav's blessing—not the inheritance of land and seed rightfully his (Gen. 28:3-4), but Esav's blessings of agricultural and political pre-eminence (Gen. 27:27-29).

Ya'akov prepares a tribute as restitution for the stolen blessing.

Ya'akov works non-stop to prepare the minchah (*tribute*)—five companies of herds, 550 animals in all! He further multiplies the gift by carefully balancing the male/female ratio to assure maximum fruitfulness for Esav's benefit.

Ya'akov tells his servants to answer Esav by saying, ". . . they are a present he has sent to my lord 'Esav" (Gen. 32:18b/19bךְ־").

Note that the word minchah (*tribute*) contains Noach (*rest*). Likewise the word machaneh (*camp*) contains chen (*favor*). Noach finds chen in the eyes of the LORD and is saved from the LORD's wrath (Gen. 6:8). Similarly, Ya'akov approaches Esav as lord, to find chen (*favor*) in Esav's sight and be saved from Esav's wrath. As restitution, Ya'akov wants to add his tribute to Esav's camp!

? Read Dt. 20:3-4. When fearing war with Esav, Ya'akov prepares (Gen. 32:7-8/8-9ךְ־"), prays (Gen. 32:9-12/10-13 ךְ־"), and presents (Gen. 32:13-21/14-22ךְ־"). Name a stress situation in your life. How should you deal with it?

Mugged

❝ Ya'akov called the place P'ni-El [face of God], "Because I have seen God face to face, yet my life has been spared." ❞

—Genesis 32:30 (31 תנ״ך)

Anxiety is so high that Ya'akov hazards a night crossing with his family (Gen. 32:22/23 תנ״ך). Then he goes back for his possessions and sends them over (Gen. 32:23/24 תנ״ך). He is left alone.

Ya'akov wrestles with God and gets renamed Yisra'el.

Suddenly—inexplicably and unexpectedly—Ya'akov is mugged!! An unknown assailant ye'avek (*wrestles*) him at the Yabok (*Jabbok River*). Ye'avek Ya'akov b'Yabok (*Jacob wrestles at the Jabbok*)!!

The wrestling match goes on all night. Ya'akov's terrific strength (Gen. 29:2-3) and his monumental perseverance are self-evident. Shortly before daybreak, the assailant touches Ya'akov's thigh with supernaturally powerful force, crippling Ya'akov!

Ya'akov is broken—he has lost everything. He cannot go forward, or Esav will kill him. He is stripped of his wives, children, servants, and possessions. Now, even his mobility is pierced. He hangs on and pleads for blessing! It comes!! Yisra'el!!!

To this day, "sons of Yisra'el" do not eat filet mignon, the sinew of the the the thigh (Gen. 32:32/33 תנ״ך). Explain the importance of preserving this memory. Why is this an appropriate first use of the term, the "sons of Yisra'el?"

Paying Tribute

" Then the slave-girls approached with their children, and they prostrated themselves; . . . **"**

—Genesis 33:6

Through word, gesture, prostration, and gifts, Ya'akov repents stealing Esav's blessing (Gen. 33:3-8, 27:27-29). After sending ahead tribute, he presents his

Concubines and children are Ya'akov's blessing.

camps.

He goes ahead of his concubines (positioned first) and his wives (second), in case he must fight [Gen. 33:3; this is his camp of refuge, Gen. 32:8/9 תנ"ך; Br. R. 78:8]. He approaches Esav with great deference, bowing low seven times (Gen. 33:3) as one would approach a monarch from afar [Amarna Letters, in Alter, p. 184]. Esav responds with an outburst of fraternal affection.

Still, Ya'akov remains deferential—always calling Esav "adoni" (*my lord*). Ya'akov seeks chen (*favor*) from his brother (Gen. 32:5/6 תנ"ך; 33:8, 10, 15). Ya'akov presses him: Kach-na et birchati (*take please my gifts, literally my blessing*). Finally, Esav gives in and accepts back the blessing (33:11). Ya'akov's mi<u>n</u>chah (*offering*) has become

Read Gen. 33:5-7. Explain why this section calls especial attention to the concubines and sons being presented.
* *Why do you suppose Ya'akov doesn't respond about the women, but does address the sons as his blessing from God?*

Shame!

❝ One time Dinah the daughter of Le'ah . . . went out to visit the local girls; and Sh'khem the son of Hamor the Hivi, the local ruler, saw her, grabbed her, raped her and humiliated her. ❞ —Genesis 34:1-2

Perhaps Dinah fails to observe a proper degree of modesty in a heathen place like Sh'chem [Rashi]. She appears to be walking around visiting houses of other women. Rachel and Rivkah appeared to have had similar freedoms (Gen. 24:16; 29:6).

The action moves quickly from Dinah seeing the daughters of the land, to Sh'chem looking lustfully upon Dinah. A fast-moving verbal chain quickens the pace (Gen. 34:2), from *saw* to *grabbed* to *lay with* (not forcibly) to *humiliated*.

The verb for *humiliated* actually does not connote rape, but rather *to take a woman without correct formalities* (Dt. 21:14; 22:24, 29).

Dinah is humiliated, with murderous consequences.

The brothers here respond to the shameful debasing of their sister with a murderous rage [Hamilton, p. 352, n5; Alter, p. 311].

Read Gen. 34:31; 49:5-7. On his deathbed, Ya'akov speaks out and curses the anger of Shim'on and Levi. Yet here he remains silent. Explain Ya'akov's behavior. Why didn't he answer his sons' retort that Dinah's honor must be upheld?

The Land Heritage

> ❝ ". . . Moreover, the land which I gave to Avraham and Yitz'chak I will give to you, and I will give the land to your descendants after you." ❞
>
> —Genesis 35:12

Heritage passes from generation to generation and never gets spent. Money passes from generation to generation and disappears. Land is a heritage, and money is an inheritance.

God gives the Land as an everlasting heritage.

Here, the Land God swore to give Avraham and Yitzchak and their seed is passed on to Ya'akov. The promise is given at Beit-El, the place where God first promised His Presence and a safe return (Gen. 28:10, 13, 15, 18-22), when VAYETSE Ya'akov (*and Jacob went out*). The journey goes full circle, as Ya'akov sets up and anoints a commemorative pillar to mark the journey's end (Gen. 35:14).

The children of Yisra'el are destined to inherit this land. They, too, must follow Ya'akov's footsteps—discarding their idols, cleansing, and changing their clothes before ascending to build the House of God (Ex. 19:10-11; Ex. 32-33; Gen. 35:2).

? *Read Gen. 35:11. Before the Land is given as an everlasting heritage, Yisra'el is told that not only a nation, but also a congregation of nations, will come from him. Explain if this includes gentile nations that can be adopted.*

Se'ir's Land First

❝ These were the descendants of Se'ir the Hori, the local inhabitants: Lotan, Shoval, Tziv'on, 'Anah, Dishon, Etzer and Dishan . . . chieftains . . . in the land of Edom. ❞   —Genesis 36:20-21

Horites possessed the Land before Esav grew into the nation of Edom and displaced them. In fact, Horites were the original inhabitants of the land of C'na'an (Gen. 14:6).

> ### Esav takes over the land of Se'ir the Horite.

Se'ir fathered seven sons (Gen. 36:20-21) as rulers, with twenty children spanning three generations. Listed above are the names of sons of the second generation (Gen. 36: 29-30). The third genera-tion sons are also listed (Gen. 36:22-28).

The Horites are succeeded by the Edomites, the sons of Esav (Gen. 36:1-19). An Edomite monarchy begins before Yisra'el has kings, with eight kings listed in Gen. 36:31-39. No dynasty is established, however, as can be inferred by the failure of fathers to pass the kingdom to their sons. The eighth king, Hadad, dies (1 Chr. 1:51), which ends the monarchy. Fragmentation comes, and a new order follows with chieftains ruling over regions.

? Read Dt. 2:2-5, 12. Explain why the LORD gave the land of Se'ir to the sons of Esav. Explain how a gradual takeover of Se'ir might account for how Esav (Edom) lived in the hills of Se'ir (Gen. 36:8-9)—later called Edom.

Edom's Land Next

" . . . *These were the chieftains of Edom according to their settlements in the land they owned. This is 'Esav the father of Edom.* **"**

—*Genesis 36:43*

Esav fails to attain an everlasting dynasty. The fathers fail to live through the sons. In fact, the line of kings never makes it to ten—a failed monarchy.

Edom dispossesses Se'ir, but not by intermarriage.

Incest is more normative in the line of Esav. Zibeon, father of Anah (Gen. 36:24) is also the brother of Anah (Gen. 36:20). He also crosses a horse with a donkey and breeds a mule (another illegitimate creature in the eyes of Torah).

According to Rashi, Timna, a granddaughter of Se'ir (the Horite) desires to intermarry Avraham's tribe— even as a concubine—so she can obtain the blessings of Avraham. Her child by Elifaz—a son, Amalek— crosses C'na'anim with the line of Esav. The resulting tribe of Amalek (Gen. 36:12; 1 Chr. 1:36) shows no fear of God, attacking the elderly and the children of Yisra'el (Dt. 25:17-18). God orders war—forever—against Amalek (Ex. 17:14-16).

? *Radak writes, "God bequeaths the earth to whomsoever He desires. For such was His will." Explain why God takes land from Canaanites and gives it to Edomites. Explain why God decrees war forever against Amalek.*

Meander

❝ Then the victorious will ascend Mount Tziyon to rule over Mount 'Esav, but the kingship will belong to ADONAI. ❞

—Obadiah 1:21

Ovadyah (*Obadiah*), the servant of the LORD, writes the above epistle as a pious Edomite governor in the palace of wicked

Edom's lust for Ya'akov's blessing will be its ruin.

King Ach'av (*Ahab*).

Picking up on the struggle between the two nations, Ovadyah prophesies that Edom's envy concerning Ya'akov's election (Gen. 27:41) will eventually bring about Edom's ruin (Ob. 1:15-18). A day will come when Edom watches—with contempt—the destruction of Y'hudah and Y'rushalayim, without lifting a hand to help his hurting brother (Ps. 137:7).

This contempt is a chilling reminder of Lemech's arrogance shortly before Kayin's line is annihilated (Gen. 4:23-24). Edom's chamas (*lawlessness*) against his brother (Ob. 1:10-11) is rooted in Hagar's chamas against Sarah (Gen. 16:5). Edom will be thrown down, and his kingdom will become the LORD's (Ob. 1:20-21). No man

? God calls a humble Edomite to prophesy the ruin of his nation. What does this say about individuals inheriting everlasting life, even if their land is lost, their seed assimilates, and the nation perishes?

...ings

" *By trusting, Yitz'chak in his blessings over Ya'akov and 'Esav made reference to events yet to come.* **"**

—Hebrews 11:20

The author of Hebrews builds on the LORD's prophecy to Rivkah (Gen. 25:23) and Yitzchak's blessing of Ya'akov (Gen. 28:3-4). Yitzchak, with eyes of faith, refers to an unseen future. Hebrews shows that the patriarchs die without experiencing the fulfillment of God's promises—rather, they salute the promises from afar.

Ya'akov bows to Edom to keep peace, reconcile, and return the blessing. But Edom will harden into a covetous nation gloating over Yisra'el's chastisement (Ob. 1:11-12).

Remember that Lot's wife lost her life by looking down upon S'dom's judgment! Similarly, Edom's gloating over the punishment of Yisra'el costs this nation its eternal life!

Edom's failure is Yisra'el's gain, only if Yisra'el is holy.

For its part, Yisra'el must stay holy to be fruitful, multiply, and fill the lands of her inheritance. Apart from obedience, Yisra'el will see the promises from afar, staying small as a people, with small needs for more land (Dt. 7:22).

? *Lot's child, Ammon, inherits C'na'ani land. Today Amman is the capital of Yarden (Jordan). Edom also forms part of Yarden. In the times of Y'hoshua (through Sh'lomo haMelech), Yisra'eli tribes lived in the land. Explain.*

Oasis

Talk Your Walk . . .

Ya'akov sends mal'achim (*messengers*) to greet Esav, but they return without ascertaining the intent of Esav, who is reportedly approaching with 400 men. Ya'akov hardly sleeps that night! In

> **Ya'akov sends all to come home.**

fact, he crosses over his wives' and concubines' camps, and then he spends the night wrestling with an unknown assailant. At dawn, stripped of all possessions and crippled as well, Ya'akov holds on for dear life and obtains the blessing—a new name, "Yisra'el," for he has striven with God and man and prevailed.

To engage Esav, Ya'akov sends ahead a huge minchah, as a tribute to soften the wrath of his brother. Ya'akov knows that the eternal land and seed inheritance is rightfully his, but he has tremendous guilt over stealing the firstborn blessing of (temporal) pre-eminence. He purposes to return the blessing, saying, "Take now, please, my blessing." Again, he prevails. He journeys on to Sukkot and then to Sh'chem, where Dinah is debased by Chamor's son, Sh'chem.

Ya'akov discards all idols and completes the return to Beit-El, the place of Ya'akov's "ladder." There, God passes on the Land as an everlasting heritage in a covenant promise. In contrast, Esav crosses out to obtain the land of Se'ir the Horite. Esav's dynasty and kingdom fail, later to be engulfed by its twin nation, Yisra'el.

...Walk Your Talk

Ya'akov's qualities of narcissistic naivete, perseverance, and naked aggression brought much tsuris (*grief*) to his life. But his covenant loyalty, and yes, truthfulness, keep him close to God and aware of God's Presence. In exile, God is "with" Ya'akov, wherever he goes. God prospers the diligent work of Ya'akov's labors; and when others (like Lavan) try to steal, God is there to defend Ya'akov.

At P'ni'el, Ya'akov is stripped of everything that he owns. He sends ahead his family! He even loses his mobility. This is crushing for a man with fight-or-flight patterns. But God is willing to break Ya'akov to straighten him out. God knows the human heart.

In that dark night at P'ni'el, Ya'akov hangs on to the one blessing he most treasures—not the temporal blessing of pre-eminence, but the eternity of God's Presence, grounded in the eternal promise of the Land. Ya'akov becomes Yisra'el that night, because he desires his

> *Blessed are the meek and lowly for they shall inherit the earth.*

highest destiny, God's dream to bring him to the Land. What dreams are you living for? How do these dreams bring light into your life and glory to the LORD God?

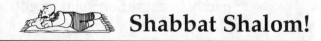 **Shabbat Shalom!**

וַיֵּשֶׁב Ya'akov settled
in the land
to continue the family line
as he planned.
But Yosef was sold,
and then he got canned!
Y'hudah intermarried,
took a Canaanite hand.

With the family in pieces
and everyone scattered,
and Yosef all beaten
and later all battered,
Y'hudah didn't think
Tamar really mattered . . .
until twins arrived
and his reputation splattered!

Walk vaYeshev!
37:1-40:23

וישב

And he settled

Ya'akov Settles
while his Family Unsettles

Hiker's Log

Looking Back

B'Reisheet (*in the beginning*), God creates a perfect paradise, and He creates man in His own image to order creation and rule over it. God's intention is that man rule as co-partner in creation, relying on God for knowledge and wisdom. But man decides to go his own way, and he obtains knowledge of good and evil for himself. Thus, man unknowingly introduces evil into the order of creation, leading to death, as God warned.

Noach (*Noah/rest*) alone finds chen (*favor*) in God's eyes. In obedience, he builds an ark to salvage a remnant from the created order. The rest are destroyed. God starts anew, with Noach as father of all mankind. It is clear that by grace man is saved, and by grace mankind is given a new chance.

Then God calls to Avram (the *exalted father*), Lech l'Cha (*go forth, yourself!*). Avram begins a faith journey on the road to a nation which God will call to covenant relationship with Himself. God renames the exalted father Avraham (*father of a multitude of nations*).

> B'Reisheet *God creates,*
> *but only* Noach *rests.*
> Lech l'Cha, *God calls to Avram.*
> vaYera—*God appears,*
> *then a miracle son.*
> Chayei Sarah *lives on*
> *through new* Tol'dot.
> vaYetse—*Ya'akov exits,*
> *sends gifts*—vaYishlach,
> vaYeshev—*and finally settles*
> *in the Land of Promise.*

To guide the building of this miracle nation, vaYera YHWH (*the Lord appeared*) to insure continuation of Chayei Sarah (*the life of Sarah*) across the Tol'dot (*generations; life* events and offspring). Twin nations are born to the successor household, **vaYetse** Ya'akov (*and out went Jacob*) to escape his brother's wrath.

But come back he must. That's when **vaYishlach** Ya'akov (*Jacob sent out*) messengers, to greet his brother and explain the 22-year absence. Ya'akov learns that Esav is coming to "greet" him with a raiding party of 400 men! That night, Ya'akov loses everything. At P'ni'el, he is renamed Yisra'el as his destiny broadens. He returns the stolen blessing to Esav, camps at Sukkot, then Sh'chem. There he buries all idols.

At Beit-El Ya'akov thanks God for a safe return by anointing a pillar, which he names Beit-El (*the House of*

In vaYeshev . . .

The Key People include Ya'akov (*Jacob*)/Yisra'el (*Israel*), Yosef (*Joseph*), brothers, Yishma'elim (*Ishmaelites*), R'uven (*Reuben*), Y'hudah (*Judah*), Potifar (*Potiphar*) and wife, Bat-Shua (*daughter of Shua*), Er, Onan, Shelah, Tamar, Peretz (*Perez*), Zerach (*Zerah*), warden, cupbearer, and baker.

The Scenes include C'na'an (*Canaan*), Sh'chem (*Shechem*), Chevron (*Hebron*), Dotan (*Dothan*), Mitzrayim (*Egypt*), and Enaim.

Main Events include Ya'akov settling; Yosef's bad report, coat, and dreams; Yosef stripped and sold twice; Y'hudah intermarried, sons killed, twins for Tamar; Yosef promoted, advances by Potifar's wife; Yosef stripped, jailed, promoted; dreams interpreted, but Yosef forgotten.

God). **vaYeshev** Ya'akov (*and Jacob settled*)—permanently, he hopes!—in the Land.

The Trail Ahead

Compass Work

The Path

וישֵׁב יעֲקֹב
בְאֶרֶץ מְגוּרֵי אבִיו
בְאֶרֶץ כְּנָעַן

—בראשית ל'ז/א

	ב	שֵׁ	יְ	וַ
letter:	vet	shin	yod	vav
sound:	V	SHeh	**Yyei**	Vah

and he settled = VAYESHEV = וישֵׁב

The Legend

<u>and settled</u> Jacob	<u>va-yeshev</u> Ya'akov	וַיֵּשֶׁב יַעֲקֹב
in the land	b'erets	בְּאֶרֶץ
journeys of father-his	m'gurei aviv	מְגוּרֵי אָבִיו
in land of Canaan	b'erets C'na'an	בְּאֶרֶץ כְּנָעַן:

—Genesis 37:1

Related Words

to sit, dwell, live, settle	yashav	יָשַׁב
to preside, be chairman (sit as head)	yashav rosh	יָשַׁב רֹאשׁ
to study under scholars (sit before wise ones)	yashav lifnei chachamim	יָשַׁב לִפְנֵי חֲכָמִים
to succeed one's father (sit on throne of father)	yashav al kise aviv	יָשַׁב עַל כִּסֵּא אָבִיו
colonizer, sitter, "squatter," (slang, buttock)	yashvan	יַשְׁבָן
settlement, population, consideration	yeeshoov	יִשּׁוּב
sedentary	yasheev	יָשִׁיב
sitting, residence, meeting, yeshiva (Talmud. college)	y'shivah	יְשִׁיבָה

Hit the Trail!

Ya'akov Settles In

> **"** *Ya'akov continued living in the land where his father had lived as a foreigner, the land of Kena'an.* **"**
>
> —*Genesis 37:1*

Home at last after more than twenty years! Ya'akov digs in! He's been away far too long—it's time to settle. VAYESHEV (*and he settled*) "where his father had lived" (Gen. 37:1) in Chevron.

Ya'akov settles in the Land, but his sons depart.

The next verse (Gen. 37:2a) continues, "Eleh tol'dot Ya'akov" (*these are the generations/life story/offspring of Ya'akov*). What follows is a fourteen-chapter story about Ya'akov's sons, and most call it the "Joseph story."

Perhaps it really is a story about Ya'akov's legacy to his sons. As Ya'akov dwells in the Land, certain events unfold in his family. Y'hudah, who is in line for the heritage blessing, descends to a Canaanite town where he intermarries. Yosef is sold for silver by his brothers and hauled down to Egypt.

Thus, even as Ya'akov tries to dig in and settle down in the Land God has sworn to give him, his family fragments and begins to assimilate.

? *Yosef lives his first 17 years at Ya'akov's house in the Land (Gen. 37:2, 28). Now read the start of VAY'CHI*
• *Ya'akov (and Jacob lived) in Gen. 47:27-28. Explain why Ya'akov will live his last 17 years at Yosef's house in Egypt.*

Yosef Ousted

> **❝** After this, when his brothers had gone to pasture their father's sheep in Sh'khem, Isra'el asked Yosef, "Aren't your brothers pasturing the sheep in Sh'khem? Come, I will send you to them." **❞** —Gen. 37:12-13a

Dotan, near Sh'chem, is the site where the brothers strip Yosef's coat from him, fling him unburied into a pit, and sell him for silver to Yishma'eli spice traders (Gen. 37:12, 17, 23-28).

> *Yosef gets ousted by his brothers, near Sh'chem.*

The brothers are alienated from Yosef by the bad reports he gives their father (Gen. 37:2), by Ya'akov's favoritism for a son of Rachel (Gen. 37:3-4), and by Yosef's pompous and narcissistic talk of dreams (Gen. 37:5-11). As a result, Yosef's ouster is assured!

The ouster sows the seeds for the prophesied exile [Gen. 15:13; Rashi, Targ. Yonatan]. The lack of brotherly love in the chosen family has been problematic from the beginning: Yishma'el vs. Yitzchak, Esav vs. Ya'akov, now Yosef vs. the brothers.

Centuries later, the sons of Yisra'el will carry out Yosef's wishes to be buried in the Land, returning his bones to another pit in nearby Sh'chem, this time for honorable burial [Gen. 50:24-25; Ex. 13:19; Josh. 24:32; Sot. 13b].

? *Read Gen. 37:4; cf. 25:28. Ya'akov understood how it felt when his father, Yitzchak, favored Esav—yet he favored Yosef anyway. Explain how Ya'akov passed on to Yosef the same jealousy that led to exile from his father's house.*

Stripped and Sold!

> **❝ So it was that when Yosef arrived to be with his brothers, they stripped off his robe, the long-sleeved robe he was wearing, and took him and threw him into the cistern . . . ❞** —Genesis 37:23-24a

What goes around, comes around! By stripping off the royal coat of Yosef, the brothers sow the seeds of Yosef's rise to pre-eminence. As they sit to eat amidst Yosef's pleas from the pit (Gen. 37:24-25; 42:21), they sow for themselves a destiny in which Yosef feasts while they cry out for help.

Y'hudah alters the plan by persuading the brothers to sell Yosef to the Yishma'elim for silver (Gen. 37:26-28). Each brother receives half a shekel in payment—thus, all bear an equal share of the sin [Stone, p. 205].

Y'hudah's move to "save" his brother will not be forgotten by the LORD (Gen. 42:21; 44:16). Selling one's brother into slavery cannot be justified merely because fratricide is avoided. Measure for measure, the brothers will be repaid for justifying Yosef's slavery on the basis of Yosef's dreams [Sforno].

The brothers sell Yosef and deceive their father.

Read Gen. 37:31-33 and recall that vaYETSE Ya'akov for 22 years. Ya'akov reaps the effects of deception when his sons present him with Yosef's blood-stained garment. Explain how Ya'akov brings a destiny of deception upon himself.

Y'hudah Goes Down!

> **“** It was at this time that Y'hudah went off from his brothers and settled near a man named Hirah who was an 'Adulami. **”**
>
> —Genesis 38:1

Y'hudah "goes down" to the royal Canaanite city of Adullam—a city that Y'hoshua will capture and make part of the tribal inheritance of Y'hudah (Josh. 12:15; 15:35). There, he joins Hirah the Canaanite in a business venture. Tradition says his status falls, because the brothers blame him for the selling of Yosef and the distress of Ya'akov [Tos. HaShalem, Tan. Yashan 8].

At Adullam, Y'hudah intermarries with the forbidden C'na'anim. Y'hudah has three sons in rapid succession. He selects a Shemite daughter [Br. R. 85:8] named Tamar to marry Er, his firstborn. God intervenes and kills Er and later Onan as well (Gen. 38:7, 10). Talmud says that both tried "to destroy seed," though for different motives [Yev.34b].

Y'hudah assimilates, but God backs it out.

Y'hudah avoids marrying Tamar to his third son Shelah, fearing a similar fate. But God has other plans. On the road to Timnah, Y'hudah fathers twins by a veiled woman more righteous than he (Gen. 38:26)!

? Read Gen. 38:7, 10. Here, the LORD takes the initiative to kill men for evil behavior. Y'hudah is "the one in whom God is praised," though he is acting otherwise. Explain why God intervenes to reverse Y'hudah's assimilation.

Yosef Bought

> " *Yosef was brought down to Egypt, and Potifar, an officer of Pharaoh's and captain of the guard, an Egyptian, bought him from the Yishma'elim who had brought him there.* " —Genesis 39:1

Alone in Egypt, vulnerable, and with a clouded future, Yosef stares at the most uncertain moment in his life [Westermann, pp. 62-68].

God is with Yosef, to bless him and Potifar, too.

However, the LORD is with Yosef (Gen. 39:2). Even as his father Ya'akov survived and prospered in exile, now Yosef experiences the blessings of God's Presence. Potifar, "He whom the god Re has given" [Hamilton, p.45], notices too.

God brings Yosef success in all that he does, and Potifar elevates Yosef to head his household (Gen. 39:3-6a; cf. Mt. 24:45-47).

Now the LORD blesses Potifar in the same ways as He had blessed Lavan. Potifar's good treatment of Yosef results in great blessing for Potiphar, too (Gen. 30:27, 30; 39:5). The LORD blesses Potifar's house, because He has promised Ya'akov, "By you and your descendants all the families of the earth will be blessed" (Gen. 28:14b; cf. Gen. 12:3).

Read Mt. 24:45-47. Does this blessing still apply today? Explain what households you care for today. What can happen when the LORD returns to put His faithful servants in charge of all His household?

Stripped Again!

> ❝ *In time, the day came when his master's wife took a look at Yosef and said, "Sleep with me!"* ❞
> —*Genesis 39:7*

Innocent and in the right, Yosef steadfastly resists the aggressive advances of Potiphar's wife (Yoma 35b). "Sleep with me!" she demands (Gen. 39: 7b, 12). Yosef resists (Gen. 39:8-9), but she uses force and seizes his garment as he flees temptation.

Yosef sidesteps adultery, but he still gets stripped.

Once again, a garment is used as evidence for a lie, with Yosef losing his most-favored position in his master's household.

This time, Yosef is cast down further, into a new house—a prison house. Each time, the pit gets deeper (Gen. 37:22, Gen. 40:15); yet always the LORD is with him (Gen. 39:21).

The blessing begins afresh! The warden of the prison notices that God is with Yosef to prosper him, and he elevates Yosef to head the prison household (Gen. 39:22-23). Yosef is neither guarded nor audited [Targ. Yonatan, cited by Stone, p. 217, n.21-23].

? *Have you lost something valuable, for wrong reasons? Yosef experienced God's Presence and prospered. Describe how you deal with frustration when unfair patterns keep playing out in your life (hint: sow for the long-term).*

Scandal!

" Some time later it came about that the Egyptian king's cupbearer and baker gave offense to thier lord the king of Egypt. "

—Genesis 40:1

Par'oh's household is scandalized! According to Rashi, first a fly is discovered in Par'oh's wine goblet—then, a pebble in Par'oh's bread basket. The fly is repulsive but harmless and could have happened after the goblet was given to Par'oh; but the pebble could have choked Par'oh, and it was obviously in the bread dough all day long [Radak].

Both the chief cupbearer and the chief baker are imprisoned for negligence—for a year [Rashi]. Both come under Yosef's care.

One night, they both dream. Yosef interprets. Par'oh "will lift up your head," he tells the chief cup-bearer. The chief cup-bearer will be counted among his courtiers (note Ex. 30:12, KI TISA, *when* the nation is *lifted up* for royal service at Sinai).

Yosef is given authority over Par'oh's stewards.

But as for the chief baker, his head will be *lifted off,* i.e. decapitated, exposed, impaled, and eaten by birds—all in three days!

? *Dreams come true. In this case, God sends dreams, and Yosef is given power to interpret the dreams. Read Gen. 40:14-15. Do you think Yosef fell short by trying to get word to Par'oh so he could get out of jail? Explain.*

The Forgotten Prophecy

> **" Nevertheless, the chief cupbearer didn't remember Yosef, but forgot him. "**
>
> —*Genesis 40:23*

orgotten! Yosef accurately interprets the dreams—giving God all the credit and all the glory (Gen. 40:8). But a gap exists between righteous acts in God's name and the workings of divine chen (*favor*).

Yosef's best efforts get him nowhere.

Yosef, it is said, placed his faith and trust in the chief cup-bearer rather than God—so God allows him to languish in jail [Sed. Olam; Tanchuma in Stone, p. 220, 15n].

For a third time, Yosef faces being forgotten. His dreams of pre-eminence and exaltation in his family seem hopelessly remote (Gen. 37:5-11); his refusal to compromise his moral standards has only gotten him jailed (Gen. 39:10, 19-20); and now his interpreting dreams to help out a fellow prisoner has been forgotten—all have gone unappreciated, falling on deaf ears.

Surely Yosef will never forget his time in jail, where he pondered whether his abilities could ever save him.

? *The path of faith and trust requires both walking and taking risks, at times, and waiting with intense prayer and hopefulness, at other times. Explain how one can know when it's best to walk, and when it's best to wait.*

Meander

❝ *The lion has roared. Who will not fear? ADONAI, God, has spoken. Who will not prophesy?* ❞

—Amos 3:8

In His grace, the LORD seeks to overlook the three sins that lead to loss of eternal life: idolatry, adultery, and murder. A nation that provides for the poor can yet borrow time, even in the face of cardinal sins.

> ## God roars, but Yisra'el sells her poor for silver.

The lion roars (Am. 3:8) over the fourth sin! God cannot countenance that Yisra'el is selling the poor for silver. In poetry, God appeals to the people (Am. 3:1-8). Punishment looms (Am. 3:13-15).

Lions roar only *after* prey is taken (Am. 3:4, 8). The poor are being preyed upon. In the courts there is no care for their guilt or innocence (Am. 2:6). Worse, clothing is taken in pledge (Am. 2:8)—a man can freeze from the cold of night when his only garment is taken. Such exploitation cannot be tolerated. God roars out His warning (Am. 3:7-8)—repent, or judgment comes swiftly (Am. 8:4). Alas, a tsadik (*righteous one*) is sold for silver [Ket. 111a], and he is Yosef [Plaut, p. 92].

? Read Ex. 21:1-2. *The foundation of Yisra'el's freedom stands on the nation's redemption from Egypt. How could Yisra'el ever forget history and exploit the poor? Explain how this behavior tests the limits of God's mercy.*

...ings

Miryam, engaged to Yosef and pregnant by a miracle of the Ruach haKodesh (*Holy Spirit*), is falsely accused of adultery. But Yosef resists the accusations, obeys God, marries, and in effect adopts Yeshua as his son in the line of Y'hudah.

Yeshua's genealogy lists only father-to-son relationships, except for 5 matriarchs and a pair of twins. Y'hudah's twin sons, Peretz and Zerach, are both listed, transcending the struggle of sibling rivalry for first-born privilege (Mt. 1:3; cf. Gen. 27:36; 4:7-11).

Astonishing parallels to Y'hudah's life appear: both Yosef and Y'hudah marry pregnant women, then abstain from relations, suffer public humiliation from the pregnancy, and begin taking action against their wives.

Yeshua comes to redeem Yisra'el's sons.

Yeshua will have many sons (Is. 53:10). The Tol'dot Yeshua (*generations of Jesus*) will include all adopted sons who resist the ways of sin and choose to become subjects of the King of kings.

? *The matriarchs (Tamar, Rachav, Rut, and Bat-Sheva) embodied sins of incest, idolatry, murder, and adultery in the Tol'dot Yeshua. Falsely accused, Miryam transcended these sins. Explain.*

Oasis

Talk Your Walk . . .

Ya'akov returns after twenty years in Charan, months in transit, and a brief stay in Sukkot. Finally, he settles into Chevron, the home and burial ground of his fathers. Ya'akov sojourns no further—like Yitzchak, he settles! He has moved enough.

But his destiny is otherwise! As Ya'akov settles in, fraternal jealousies erupt. Paternal favoritism and Yosef's apparently self-serving dreams of grandeur (at the brothers' and even parents' expense) sharpen sibling rivalries to the breaking point.

Ya'akov's foothold in the Land will not endure. Yosef is sold for silver and taken down to Egypt as a slave. Y'hudah intermarries, following Esav's footsteps toward assimilation. But even as Ya'akov's family fragments, Yosef is sowing seeds for salvation. Falsely accused, he is first enslaved by his brothers, then imprisoned by the Egyptians.

> *Ya'akov settles while his family unsettles.*

Yosef, however, walks closely with the LORD. Because Yosef abides with God, everything he attempts prospers. Whether in Potifar's house or in an Egyptian prison, Yosef will be promoted to head the household. In time, the tables of misfortune will turn. Yosef will hold the power to enslave and imprison not only his family, but also Egypt, the world empire.

...Walk Your Talk

Does trying matter with God or not? Some say that all our righteousness is filthy rags and that no one can merit anything from God. Others say that you have not because you ask not, and that you must walk in faith to get anywhere. Is there an answer?

Yosef forgot to give God credit for the dreams he shared with his brothers. After nearly twelve years of pondering in exile and in jail, his moment came! Par'oh's chief cupbearer and chief baker dream dreams, which Yosef accurately interprets. This time, he is especially careful to assign all credit to God!

Yosef also takes the initiative with the chief cupbearer, whom he accurately predicts will be set free in three days. Yosef slips in a plea for a good word to Par'oh. He confidently waits for things to happen.

What could possibly go wrong? He's been unfairly sold for silver, unfairly charged with making advances, and unfairly left to languish in jail for no reason at all. Now he sees God acting through dreams and knows he's

> *God purifies hearts to give Him all glory.*

about to get out. Why must he then wait for another set of dreams, which will come two years later?

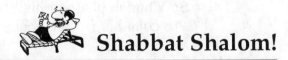

Shabbat Shalom!

At the end of—מִקֵּץ—
after two more years,
Joe explained the dreams
about cows 'n ears.
Made second to Pharaoh—
oh, how he beamed!
Then his brothers bowed down,
just like he dreamed!

Forced by the famine
to beg for food,
they figured Joe was
an Egyptian dude.
But he said, "Go home!
Don't come back without Ben!"
So Y'hudah pledged his life
to calm his father again.

Walk MiKETZ!
41:1-44:17

מִקֵּץ

At the end of

TORAH—Genesis 41:1-44:17
- 1st The End of a Nightmare—Genesis 41:1
- 2nd Par'oh's Nightmare—Genesis 41:15
- 3rd The Dreamer Interprets—Genesis 41:39-40a
- 4th The Nightmare Plays Out—Genesis 41:53-54a
- 5th Starving Brothers—Genesis 42:19
- 6th Feast During Famine—Genesis 43:16
- 7th Weeping in Secret—Genesis 43:30
- Maftir Nightmare for Ya'akov—Genesis 44:17

HAFTARAH—1 Kings 3:15-4:1
- A Nightmare Decision—I Kings 3:28b-4:1

B'RIT CHADASHAH—Matthew 27:15-46
- Yeshua's Nightmare—Matthew 27:46

At the End of the Nightmare,
Dreams Come True!

Hiker's Log

 Looking Back

B'REISHEET (*in the beginning*), God creates paradise. Man is told to be fruitful, multiply, fill the earth, and subdue it. But man disobeys, choosing exile, destruc-

> **B'REISHEET** *God creates.*
> *Only* **NOACH** *rests.*
> *God calls,* **LECH L'CHA.**
> *Then* **VAYERA!**
> *God announces Yitzchak.*
> **CHAYEI SARAH** *continues through* **TOL'DOT.**
> **VAYETSE**—*Ya'akov exits, sends gifts—**VAYISHLACH,** and resettles—**VAYESHEV.***
> *But Yosef* <u>unsettles</u>
> *'til* **MIKETZ**—*at the end of two more years . . .*

tion, and death.

First, Adam is banished from Gan Eden; later, although **NOACH** (*Noah/rest*) rests, corporate mankind dies in the flood. Mankind resists divine plans again, choosing instead

to unify at Bavel in Shin'ar and take heaven by force. The LORD frustrates man's tower building efforts, introducing language diversity and separate nations.

God calls out to one man, **LECH L'CHA** (*go forth, yourself!*). Avram begins his faith journey to the Promised Land and circumcises his entire international household.

VAYERA YHWH (*and the LORD appeared*) three days later, announcing that the matriarch—yes, Sarah!—will mother a miracle son as Avraham's heir. The LORD's angel "appears" again at the future temple site, Moriah, announcing Avraham will become father to an indestructible nation through Yitzchak, son of the covenant promise.

CHAYEI SARAH (*the life of Sarah*) continues the covenant promises to the next generation. **Tol'dot** (*generations*) extend the land and seed heritage to Yitzchak's household and beyond. **vaYetse** Ya'akov (*and Jacob went out*) to his ancestral home at Charan (faith's *crossroads*), to find a Shemite wife and escape the wrath of his twin brother. Ya'akov's sin of stealing his brother's blessing will separate him from his father for 22 years. Returning to the land, **vaYishlach** (*and he sent*) tribute to reconcile with Esav. But first, he is broken at P'ni'el by a divine messenger who renames him Yisra'el.

vaYeshev Ya'akov (*and Jacob settled*), staking his claim to the Promised Land. His sons drift off, however. Yosef is sold for silver, exiled for 22 years, and presumed dead. Y'hudah assimilates in a Canaanite town. Even

---

In miKetz . . .

The Key People include Par'oh (*Pharaoh*), his cupbearer, Yosef (renamed Tsaf'nat-Pa'neach), wife Os'nat (*Asenath*)—daughter of Potifera, M'nasheh (*Manasseh*), Efrayim (*Ephraim*), Ya'akov, and the eleven sons.

The Scenes include haY'or (*the Nile*), Mitzrayim (*Egypt*), and C'na'an (*Canaan*).

The Main Events include Par'oh's dream, Yosef's interpretation, new job preparing for famine, brothers' visit, Shim'on jailed, request to see Binyamin, second visit, trap to frame Binyamin with stolen cup, the chase and accusation, and Binyamin sentenced to die.

Ya'akov's efforts to hold on to Binyamin, the only living memory of his beloved Rachel, will be tested before the nightmare ends. But **miKetz** (*at the end*), when Yosef is sprung from jail, ancient dreams begin to come

The Trail Ahead ➡

Compass Work

The Path

ויהי מקץ שנתים ימים
ופרעה חלם
והנה עמד על היאר

—בראשית מא/א

צ	קֶ	מִ
letter:		
tsadee sofeet	koof	mem
sound:		
TS	**Kkei**	Mee

at the end of = MIKETZ = מקץ

The Legend

and it was <u>at the end of</u>	va-y'hi mikets	וַיְהִי מִקֵּץ
two years of days	sh'natayim yamim	שְׁנָתַיִם יָמִים
that Pharaoh dreamed	oo-far'oh cholem	וּפַרְעֹה חֹלֵם
and here	v'hinei	וְהִנֵּה
stood	omed	עֹמֵד
on the Nile River . . .	al-ha-y'or	עַל־הַיְאֹר:

—Gen. 41:1

Related Words

end, destruction (Gen. 6:13, Ps. 119:96)	kets	קֵץ
after, at the end of	mikets	מִקֵּץ
at the end of	l'kets	לְקֵץ
from time to time, now and then	l'kitsim	לְקִצִּים
his end has come (arrived)	ba (higia) kitso	בָּא (הִגִּיעַ) קִצּוֹ
reckoners of the end of days, eschatologists	m'chashvei kitsin	מְחַשְּׁבֵי קִצִּין
cut off, chop, destroy	katsats	קָצַץ
severance of family con- nection, selling heir- loom to outsider, mar- rying social inferior	k'tsatsah	קְצָצָה

Hit the Trail!

The End of a Nightmare

> **" At the end of two years, Pharaoh had a dream: he was standing beside the Nile River . . . "**
>
> —*Genesis 41:1*

iterally *at the end of two years of days*, God sends a pair of prophetic dreams to Par'oh. Yosef, nearly thirty, has spent almost twelve years in jail.

This time, a pair of dreams springs Yosef from the pit.

The nightmarish quality of the dreams deeply disturbs Par'oh's spirit (Gen. 41:8). Par'oh knows well that the Nile is the source of Egypt's prosperity and stability. He can't shake the ominous picture of foul-looking cows, ugly and gaunt (Gen. 41:3), turning carnivorous and cannibalizing the fatted cows that stood at the banks of the Nile.

The dreams are not interpreted in a way that satisfies [Rashi, on Gen. 41:8]. Pressure builds in the court. Finally, the chief cupbearer "remembers" that Yosef is able to interpret dreams (Gen. 41:9-13). Par'oh sends immediately for Yosef, who is hurried from the pit and quickly given a change of garments and a fresh shave!

? *Rosh haShanah 10b says that Yosef is sprung from prison on Rosh haShanah. Read 1 Thess. 4:13-17. Explain how Yosef, the dead in Messiah, and those who await the Messiah share a similar hope, dream, and redemption.*

Par'oh's Nightmare

> **"** *Pharaoh said to Yosef, "I had a dream, and there is no one who can interpret it; but I've heard it said about you that when you hear a dream, you can interpret it."* **"**
>
> —Genesis 41:15

Par'oh tells Yosef that "no one can interpret" his dreams (Gen. 41:15). These are the exact words that the chief cupbearer and now-deceased baker told Yosef two years earlier (Gen. 40:8).

Yosef does not respond, "Relate it to me," as he said previously. Two additional years in prison (measured in days) have broken Yosef's confidence in his abilities. Now, Yosef answers that it is beyond him. Yosef refuses to accept the inference that he has supernatural powers [Stone, p. 225; Mizrachi]. He follows up his disclaimer, adding, "God will answer."

Par'oh's dreams are beyond Yosef.

Par'oh then relates his dreams. Yosef answers that the "second" dream is a punctuating of the first dream, indicating a single dream that God will fulfill quickly (Gen. 41:32). Cows stand for years in Egyptian inscriptions [Fox, p. 192]—so Yosef forecasts seven years of plenty followed by seven years of famine.

> **?** *Read Gen. 41:8, 38. Note that Yosef amazes Par'oh because Ruach Elohim bo (the Spirit of God is in him).*
> • *What does Torah mean, when Par'oh tells his court that Yosef is spirit-filled?*

The Dreamer Interprets

> **❝ So Pharaoh said to Yosef, "Since God has shown you all this—there is no one as discerning and wise as you—you will be in charge of my household ... ❞**
> —Genesis 41:39-40a

Par'oh echoes Yosef's words that all interpretations come from God. Then he promotes Yosef to head the largest household in Egypt! Par'oh gives Yosef his signet ring, the royal seal-bearer for signing documents with Par'oh's authority, and robes of shesh (*fine linen*), the same material as the garments given later to the Levitical priests.

Yosef's rise is a stunning display—since Egyptian law forbids foreign slaves from ruling or wearing the robes of a noble! The astrologers protested,

"Will you set over us a slave whose master bought him for 20 pieces of silver?" [Sot. 36b].

Yosef is promoted to head Par'oh's household.

Par'oh overrules, exalting Yosef to the viceroy position and assigning him the second royal chariot. Par'oh gives him a new name, Tsaf'nat-Pa'neach (*The God speaks, and He lives*) [Fox, p. 188]. Finally, in a smashing vindication of his sexual purity, Yosef is given Potifar's daughter to wed [Stone, p. 229].

? Read Romans 8:28. God redeems Yosef's failed effort to use dream interpretation to get in a good word with Par'oh. Explain how Yosef's tears from unfulfilled dreams and false charges are changed to tears of great joy.

The Nightmare Plays Out

> **"** *The seven years of abundance in the land of Egypt ended; and the seven years of famine began to come, just as Yosef had said . . .* **"**
> —Genesis 41:53-54a

Years of plenty end with the birth of Yosef's two sons (Gen. 41:51-52)—M'nasheh (*God has made me forget* all my hardship and my father's house) and Efrayim (*God has made me fruitful* in the land of my suffering).

> ## Yosef is remembered for predicting severe famine.

Then, the second shoe drops. Par'oh's nightmare plays out as suffering increases dramatically, and Yosef is credited with the forecast (Gen. 41:54).

The famine is chazak (*strong, severe*)—the term used twice here (Gen. 41:56-57), but elsewhere only to describe conditions during the fall of Y'rushalayim (2 Ki. 25:3). The extent of the famine is global. "Kol" (*all*) is used 11 times (Gen. 41:48, 51, 54, 55, 56), culminating with "kol ha'aretz" (*all the earth*) twice (Gen. 41:57).

The famine is an anti-flood epoch. Severe drought keeps the Nile from flooding [Wenham, p. 398]. The following year, food shortages drive the people to seek Yosef, for relief.

? *Read Gen. 42:2, 18. Explain how the life and death situation introduced by the famine affects Ya'akov and his sons in Yisra'el. Note also Gen. 43:8, 47:19. Explain what "live and not die" means in each context.*

Starving Brothers

Jailed as spies, the brothers are released. Compassion from the viceroy of Egypt allows the brothers to return home with grain for their starving families (Gen. 42:19).

This compassion stirs feelings of guilt in the brothers. Now they remember how Yosef pleaded from the pit, while they sat eating in callous disregard, offering him no food (Gen. 42:21-22).

In Hebrew, the brothers discuss their guilt among themselves. No one knows that Yosef can understand.

Their admission of guilt and fear of judgment move Yosef to withdraw, where he secretly sheds tears. Then he returns and jails Shim'on (Gen. 42:24).

Next trip, the brothers must bring Binyamin.

Yosef requires them to bring Binyamin in order to verify their honesty. He reasons that the brothers cannot get a stranger to risk his life posing as the younger brother [Sforno].

? *Y'hudah, like Ya'akov, has lost two children (Gen. 38:7, 10). Read Gen. 43:9. Explain why Y'hudah tells Ya'akov that he will personally guarantee Binyamin's life. Why does Ya'akov find this offer more compelling than R'uven's?*

Feast During Famine

❝ When Yosef saw Binyamin with them, he said to his household manager, "Take the men inside the house, kill the animals and prepare the meat. These men will dine with me at noon." ❞ —Genesis 43:16

When supplies dwindle, Y'hudah prevails. Ya'akov releases Binyamin to make the second trip and advises his sons to return with money in hand and a minchah (*tribute*) (Gen. 43:11-15).

Yosef's household feasts while the world fasts.

Yosef's servant invites the brothers to a meal in the private palace of Yosef. The brothers show up, with the tribute and money b'yadam (*in their hands*) (Gen. 43:26, cf. 43:12, 15). They bow before Yosef—here is the fulfillment of Yosef's first dream, twenty-two years before (Gen. 37:7)! The brothers' need for grain completes the dream of the brothers' sheaves bowing to Yosef's.

This scene calls to mind breathtaking parallels to the time when vaYishlach Ya'akov (*and Jacob sent*): Ya'akov bows before Esav, sends a tribute ahead, approaches Esav as a monarch, and attempts to return the firstborn blessing of pre-eminence (Gen. 32:3ff/4ff תנ״ך; 1 Chr. 5:1-2).

? *Read Gen. 43:33-34. Explain why the brothers are seated according to age and yet the youngest receives a portion five times larger than the others. In what way does this meal symbolize the firstborn blessing passing to Yosef?*

Weeping in Secret

> **"** *Then Yosef hurried out, because his feelings toward his brother were so strong that he wanted to cry; he went into his bedroom and there he wept.* **"**
> —Genesis 43:30

Yosef weeps twice in this portion (Gen. 42:24; 43:30) and twice in the next portion (Gen. 45:2, 14-15). The tough, hardened viceroy of Egypt shows particularly intense emotion over reuniting with his brother Binyamin, Rachel's youngest. Yet Yosef weeps again in secret, to complete the testing of the brothers.

Yosef weeps in secret, so he can test his brothers.

The first test occurs at the meal, when Binyamin receives the largest portions and special attention. The brothers react by drinking heavily and getting intoxicated (Gen. 43:34). Yosef takes opportunity to stuff their bags with silver; then he orders his divination cup pressed into Binyamin's sack (Gen. 44:1-2).

In the second test, Yosef develops a situation where Binyamin will be imprisoned, unless the brothers act to free him. The brothers exhibit t'shuvah (*repentance*), replacing hostile patterns of sibling rivalry with loving patterns of brotherly care. In Kayin, sibling rivalry triumphed. Here, brothers stick together!

> **?** At Dotan, the brothers tore Yosef's clothes, disregarded his pleadings, and sold him (Gen. 37:23, 28, 42:21). When Binyamin is taken, the brothers tear their own clothes (Gen. 44:8-13). Explain the brothers' awakening to t'shuvah.

Nightmare for Ya'akov

> **"** But he replied, "Heaven forbid that I should act in such a way. The man in whose possession the goblet was found will be my slave; but as for you, go in peace to your father. **"**
> —Genesis 44:17

Nightmares abound! Par'oh's nightmare is that Egypt will be pressed hard with a severe famine (Gen. 41:1-7). R'uven's nightmare is that the brothers will be punished for shedding innocent blood (Gen. 42:22). The brothers' nightmare is that Yosef will receive preeminence (Gen. 37:8).

Ya'akov's nightmare comes true.

Ya'akov's nightmare is that Binyamin will descend and never return from Egypt (Gen. 42:38; 43:13-14). To spare his father unprecedented anguish, Y'hudah promises to pledge his life for Binyamin's.

Here, Yosef's servant searches the brother's bags, asking a question eerily similar to the one asked by Lavan—where is Yosef's divining cup? Remember that Ya'akov inadvertently cursed Rachel, when he said that whoever took Lavan's idols should die (Gen. 31:32). The brothers make the same pledge, and the cup turns up in Binyamin's sack!

? Consider how long Yosef waited: a year with Potifar, twelve years in jail, nine years as viceroy. More than 22 years passed before Yosef's first dream came true. What does this say about how God teaches patience to His sons?

Meander

" All Isra'el heard of the decision the king had made and held the king in awe, for they saw that God's wisdom was in him . . . King Shlomo was king over all Isra'el. " —1 Kings 3:28-4:1

The Torah portion is preceded by Yosef's dreams that his brothers will bow down to him. The Haftarah is preceded by a dream in which Sh'lomo asks ADONAI for wisdom to rule.

ADONAI exalts those whose hearts are right with Him.

The test comes immediately. At a feast, two harlots approach the young king, both claiming to be the mother of a certain newborn. Each insists that the other's infant died during the night.

Sh'lomo rules that the living child should be divided and half given to each woman. The true mother "yearns" for her child's life. Her display of compassion contrasts sharply with the cold response of the other, who is satisfied to see the child cut in two. Sh'lomo rules a second time for the child to be given to the woman who shows love. The people fear in awe for their king, because they see the wisdom of God at work in him (1 Ki. 3:28).

Read 1 Kings 3:5-7, 10-14. Does the LORD still approach individuals in dreams? The dreams of Yosef and Sh'lomo were fulfilled when they selflessly glorified God. How can you prepare your heart to approach God selflessly?

...ings

> **At about three, Yeshua uttered a loud cry, "Eli! Eli! L'mah sh'vaktani? (My God! My God! Why have you deserted me?)"**
>
> —*Matthew 27:46*

What could be worse than separation from God the Father? At Gat-Sh'manim (*Gethsemane*), Yeshua prayed that His cup of suffering be removed, but surrendered His will to the Father (Mt. 26:39).

The Lamb takes upon himself our sins and is cut off from God.

It was customary before Passover for the imperial magistrate of Rome to acquit or pardon a prisoner charged with a capital crime. Jewish Law permitted slaughter of a korban pesach (*Passover Lamb*) for those unable to partake--- the terminally ill or sentenced to die [M. Pes. 8:6].

Pilate's wife dreams that Yeshua is not deserving of crucifixion (Mt. 27:19), and she warns her husband. But the crowd demands the release of Yeshua Bar Abba (*Barabbas/lit. Jesus, Son of the Father*)—a popular nationalist and insurrectionist (Jn. 18:40; Lk. 23:14-19; Ac. 3:14).

Darkness descends on the Land. Then Yeshua, the King of the Jews, is cut off from God the Father.

? *The crowd wanted a nation, free from Rome. Barabbas was their hero, an insurrectionist trying to throw off the Roman yoke. If Rome really understood God's kingdom, would Yeshua die for the crime of insurrection? Explain.*

Oasis

Talk Your Walk . . .

Yosef spends two more years in the pit after correctly interpreting the dreams of the chief cupbearer and the baker. Yosef silently learns that perfect effort on his part will not free him to pursue his dreams. Though Yosef is forgotten by man, he is not forgotten by God. Two years later to the day, God sends a pair of nightmares to Par'oh. Yosef alone is given "discernment and wisdom" to correctly interpret the dreams. Yosef immediately is lifted up from jail and exalted with a royal coat, a new name, and marriage to the daughter of the one who accused him!

> *At the end of the nightmare, dreams come true!*

Par'oh's dreams come to pass as foretold by God and interpreted by Yosef. Seven years of plenty are followed by a dire worldwide famine. In fact, Yosef's brothers are driven from C'na'an in search of food. The tables are turned. Yosef sees the brothers coming and accuses them of spying against him! To test their honesty, he jails Shim'on. He tells them sternly to return with Binyamin. But losing the last son of Rachel is a living nightmare for Ya'akov. Y'hudah promises to safeguard Binyamin with his own life.

All brothers return to Yosef, bowing for food. A feast is prepared, and Binyamin receives quintuple portions. Yosef maintains his disguise, weeping in private. But he lays a trap, planting his silver cup in the sack of Binyamin, his brother.

. . . Walk Your Talk

Yosef's test is Y'hudah's worst nightmare. The Egyptians find the silver divining cup in Binyamin's sack and haul him back to jail. To separate Ya'akov from his beloved son Binyamin will send his father's white head down to Sh'ol (*abode of the dead*) in grief (Gen. 42:38).

In another age, Sh'lomo haMelech offered to cut a child in two to arbitrate a dispute. Moreover, ADONAI actually endured (in fact "was pleased") that His son become an asham (*guilt offering*) for our sins (Is. 53:10). When Yeshua died, He and His Father were cut off from one another. In this way, God faced His worst nightmare. And He faced it out of love for man!

What is *your* worst nightmare? What are your deepest fears? Do not deceive yourself into thinking that your fears will remain a secret! God loves you far too much to leave secrets hidden away in your heart. Your

> *Facing up to nightmares is the road to salvation.*

secrets are known, and your life is predestined to bring you face to face with your worst fears.

How can you prepare for such a time? Y'hudah prepared by repenting of the evil he caused his father. You can face up by being honest and committing all fears to God. Ask yourself, are you ready to face up?

Shabbat Shalom!

וַיִּגַּשׁ Y'hudah, he drew near
to the viceroy
and pleaded,
"Please, Sir, spare the boy!
Our father, Old Ya'akov,
will die without joy
if Benjamin's
not in our convoy.

Instead take *my* life,
'cuz Ben's no cad!"
Then the viceroy cried out,
"Come close! I'm not mad!
I'm the one whom you sold—
Brother Joe! Don't feel bad!!
Go home with great news!
Come back with our dad!"

Walk vaYigash!
44:18-47:27

And he drew near

TORAH—Genesis 44:18-47:27
- 1st Drawing Near—Genesis 44:18
- 2nd Offering Self—Genesis 44:31
- 3rd Reconciled with God—Genesis 45:8
- 4th Royal Welcome—Genesis 45:19
- 5th Father United—Genesis 45:28
- 6th Family United—Genesis 46:28-29a
- 7th Land—Genesis 47:11
- Maftir Multiplying a Nation—Genesis 47:27

HAFTARAH—Ezekiel 37:15-28
- The Nation Sanctified—Ezekiel 37:28

B'RIT CHADASHAH—Luke 6:12-16
- Growing God's Kingdom—Luke 6:16

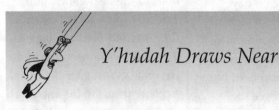

Y'hudah Draws Near

Hiker's Log

← Looking Back

B'REISHEET *(in the beginning)*, God creates paradise. He tells man to be fruitful, multiply, fill the earth, and subdue it. Instead, man disobeys, choosing a path that leads to exile, destruction, and death. But God purposes to redeem man. NOACH *(Noah/rest)* rests, and God begins anew—giving him seventy sons, who become the nations of the world. The nations try to unify at Shin'ar to take heaven by force.

God counters by calling LECH L'CHA *(go forth, yourself!)*. Avram becomes Avraham, *the father of a multitude of nations.* God purposes to reach the nations of the world through a new nation. VAYERA YHWH *(and the LORD appeared)*—not only to announce the miracle birth of Avraham's son and heir; but also later to preserve the

embodied hope of resurrection in Yitzchak, offered up at Moriah. There, God tells Avraham his seed will mature into an indestructible nation.

> **B'REISHEET** *God creates.*
> *Only* **NOACH** *rests.*
> *God calls,* **LECH L'CHA.** *Then*
> **VAYERA!** *God announces Yitzchak.*
> **CHAYEI SARAH** *continues*
> *through new* **TOL'DOT.**
> **VAYETSE, VAYISHLACH,**
> **VAYESHEV—**
> *Ya'akov exits, sends gifts, resettles.*
> *But Yosef* <u>unsettles</u>
> *'til* **MIKETZ**—*at the end,*
> *dreams come true and*
> *Y'hudah draws near—***VAYIGASH!**

CHAYEI SARAH *(the life of Sarah)* continues the household to the next generation. TOL'DOT *(generations)* extend the land and seed heritage to Yitzchak, his household, and beyond. VAYETSE Ya'akov *(and Jacob went out)* to his ancestral home, to escape Esav's wrath and avoid assimilation in C'na'an. Later, **VAYISHLACH** Ya'akov *(and Jacob sent)* tribute to reconcile with his twin brother. Then, having learnt his lesson, **VAYESHEV** Ya'akov *(and Jacob settled)* in the Land.

His family drifts off, however—Yosef is sold for silver, and Y'hudah intermarries. Meanwhile, **MIKETZ** *(at the end of)* a long time in jail, Yosef gets elevated to viceroy of Egypt. There he forces his hungry brothers to face past sins. **VAYIGASH** Y'hudah *(and Judah drew near)* to face down the prospect of sinning against his father again. In a royal and selfless way, Y'hudah pledges his own life as surety that Binyamin will not follow his brother's footsteps to an Egyptian jail. The

In VAYIGASH . . .

The Key People include Y'hudah *(Judah)*, Yosef *(Joseph)*, the brothers, Ya'akov *(Jacob)*, Par'oh *(Pharaoh)*, and the sons (66 people in all).

The Scenes include Goshen, Mitzrayim *(Egypt)*, C'na'an *(Canaan)*, B'er Shava *(Beersheba)*, and the district of Rameses.

The Main Events include Y'hudah drawing near to Yosef to take Binyamin's place, Yosef revealing his identity, brothers returning to get Ya'akov, God reassuring Ya'akov on trip to Egypt, sons listed, Par'oh giving family the best land in Goshen, the famine continuing with Egyptians selling Yosef their livestock and land . . . til all are indebted to Par'oh and Yosef.

portion ends with Yisra'el settled in Egypt. God's original purposes for mankind are evident—His nation is fruitful and multiplying exceedingly!

The Trail Ahead

Compass Work

The Path

וַיִּגַּשׁ אֵלָיו יְהוּדָה וַיֹּאמֶר
בִּי אֲדֹנִי יְדַבֶּר נָא עַבְדְּךָ
דָבָר בְּאָזְנֵי אֲדֹנִי
וְאַל יִחַר אַפְּךָ בְּעַבְדֶּךָ
כִּי כָמוֹךָ כְּפַרְעֹה

—בראשית מד/יח

	ש	גַ	יִ	וַ
letter:	shin	gimmel	yod	vav
sound:	SH	**Ggah**	Yyee	Vah

and he drew near = VAYIGASH = וַיִּגַּשׁ

The Legend

<u>and drew near</u> to him	*va-**yigash*** elav	וַיִּגַּשׁ אֵלָיו
Judah	*Y'hudah*	יְהוּדָה
and said oh lord-my	*va-**yomer** bi adoni*	וַיֹּאמֶר בִּי אֲדֹנִי
let speak please	*y'daber-**na***	יְדַבֶּר־נָא
servant-your a word	*av'd'cha **davar***	עַבְדְּךָ דָבָר
in ears of lord-my	*b'oznei adoni*	בְּאָזְנֵי אֲדֹנִי
and not flare nose-your	*v'al-**yichar** ap'**cha***	וְאַל־יִחַר אַפְּךָ
(become angry) at servant-your	*b'av'decha*	בַּעַבְדֶּךָ
because like you	*ki chamocha*	כִּי כָמוֹךָ
like Pharaoh	*k'far'oh*	כְּפַרְעֹה:

—*Genesis 44:18*

Related Words

to approach, come near, begin, start, set to	*nigash*	נִגַּשׁ
to bring near, present, offer	*higish*	הִגִּישׁ
to collide, come into conflict with, draw near	*hitnagesh*	הִתְנַגֵּשׁ
to present a gift	*higish matanah*	הִגֵּשׁ מַתָּנָה
to submit a report (present judgm't & accting)	*higish din v'cheshbon*	הִגֵּשׁ דִּין־וְחֶשְׁבּוֹן

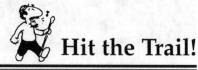

Hit the Trail!

Drawing Near

❝ *Then Y'hudah approached Yosef and said, "Please, my lord! Let your servant say something to you privately; and don't be angry with your servant, for you are like Pharaoh himself."* ❞   —*Genesis 44:18*

Walking the road to t'shuvah (*repentance*), Y'hudah draws near to Yosef. He must offer himself for Binyamin to honor his personal pledge to his father (Gen. 44:32). Ironically, Y'hudah must offer to take his brother's place in solemnity and humility.

> *Y'hudah steps forward to reconcile with Yosef.*

In the longest speech of Genesis, Y'hudah carefully avoids creating offense, even in minor ways. He honors Ya'akov's favoritism for the sons of Rachel (Gen. 37:3-4), explaining how important Binyamin is to his father (Gen. 44:20, 29-31). He embraces Rachel's last son as a brother, calling the son of Rachel *achinu* (*our brother* in Gen. 43:4). He honors the viceroy as Par'oh himself, unknowingly showing proper deference to Yosef (Gen. 44:18). He is even prepared to accept Leah, his mother, as a less loved wife—though, at some level, Ya'akov's favoritism must make him feel like a second-class son of Leah (Gen. 42:38).

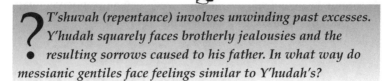

T'shuvah (repentance) involves unwinding past excesses. Y'hudah squarely faces brotherly jealousies and the resulting sorrows caused to his father. In what way do messianic gentiles face feelings similar to Y'hudah's?

Offering Self

" . . . *when he sees that the boy isn't with us, he will die; and your servants will bring the gray hair of your servant our father down to Sh'ol with grief.* **"**
—*Genesis 44:31*

Echoing the conscience of his father, Y'hudah squarely faces the grief he once caused his father by returning without Yosef (Gen. 37:26-28, 34-35; cf. Gen. 42:38).

Y'hudah offers himself in selfless, loving repentance.

This time, he plunges headlong into the path of loving, selfless sacrifice, offering to stay as slave in place of Binyamin (Gen. 44:32-33). He implores the viceroy (who secretly watches him through the eyes of Yosef, his brother):

Let me not see the evil that will find my father! In later times, Yeshua will say the greatest love is shown when a person "lays down his life for his friends" (John 15:13).

Yosef's eyes pop out of his head. As viceroy, he clears the room. Then, standing alone with his brothers, Yosef bursts into loud, uncontrollable weeping that can be heard through the walls and throughout all Egypt (Gen. 45:2). Finally, he tells his brothers: Ani Yosef! Ha'od avi chai? (*I am Joseph! Is my father still alive?*)

? "So, too, will it be in the time to come when God will reveal Himself and announce, 'I am HASHEM!' The veil will be lifted from our eyes and we will comprehend . . ." [Chafetz Chaim in Stone, p. 253]. Comprehend what? Explain.

Reconciled with God

> **"** *So it was not you who sent me here, but God; and he has made me a father to Pharaoh, lord of all his household and ruler over the whole land of Egypt.* **"** —*Genesis 45:8*

Brothers stand in silent, stunned incredulity. Yosef tries again: G'shu-na elai. (*Come close now, please, to me!*)

Now the brothers draw near, and Yosef goes on (Gen. 45:4-5): Ani Yosef achichem, asher m'chartem otee Mitzraimah. (*I am Yosef your brother, whom you sold into Egypt.*) Do not be distressed, nor angry with yourselves that you sold me here, for it's a m'chiyah (*life saver*) that God sent me here ahead of you.

Yosef continues to talk (Gen. 45:6-13), but there is no response from the brothers. Finally, he falls on Binyamin's neck, kissing him, and then does likewise with all his brothers (Gen. 45:14-15). His affection breaks the ice.

> *Yosef reassures his brothers that God is redeeming.*

But Yosef's words are more than prattle. Yosef reassures his brothers that God's hand is at work. The famine will continue for five more years; so the brothers must go to C'na'an for dad, then return and stay close to Yosef.

? *Meditate on Gen. 44:18; 45:4, 5-13, 14-15. Y'hudah initiates drawing near, triggering a response from Yosef.*
● *Y'hudah offers himself, and then Yosef reveals himself. What initiatives precede lasting reconciliation?*

Royal Welcome

> ❝ *"Moreover—and this is an order—do this: take wagons from the land of Egypt to carry your little ones and your wives, and bring your father, and come."* ❞ —Genesis 45:19

Par'oh conveys a formal welcome to Ya'akov with a command to pave the way for his journey (cf. Ya'akov's formal greeting to Esav, Gen. 32:4-5/5-6 הנד"ך).

Yosef sends a royal escort to usher Yisra'el to Egypt.

Ya'akov's age and resistance to leaving C'na'an are causes for concern. For this reason, Yosef sends wagons as a seal of the royal escort. In fact, Par'oh's invitation to settle in the fertile area of Goshen, along with gifts of clothing, silver, donkeys, and food, confers royal status on the family [Sarna; Gen. 45:19-23].

The plan for a royal welcome and escort works. Initially as dumfounded and incredulous as the brothers once were, Ya'akov revives (lit., *and the spirit of Ya'akov lived*) when he sees the wagons (Gen. 45:27). Speaking as head of the nation (Gen. 45:28a), Yisra'el responds: Rav 'od Yosef b'ni chai! El'chah. (*Great! Still Joseph my son lives!! I shall go.*) So the family, a nation-in-embryo, walks the long, winding journey to nationhood (Gen. 15:13-14).

? *Read Gen. 24:58, 45:26-28. Recall that Rivkah mothers two nations in her womb, after an escort to the place where the nations will be born. Explain how the spirit of Ya'akov is revived so that Yisra'el makes the journey.*

Father United

❝ Isra'el said, "Enough! My son Yosef is still alive! I must go and see him before I die." ❞

—Genesis 45:28

Ya'akov packs up and heads south. At B'er Shava, he stops and offers sacrifices to the God of Yitzchak. That night, God speaks to him in a prophetic vision, telling him not to fear going down to Egypt, for God will make him a great nation there. In fact, God says: anochi ered imcha (*I will go down with you*), v'anochi a'alcha gam a'lot (*and I will also bring you back up*) with the new nation (Gen. 46:1-4). In this way, God comforts Ya'akov with His presence and with a promise.

God's endorsement, encouragement, and promise of a safe return echo past promises when VAYETSE Ya'akov (*Jacob went out*) from the Land and he came back safely as promised (Gen. 28:15, 20; 35:1, 3, 9, 15).

> *Ya'akov exits the Land, this time to start a nation.*

Ya'akov sets out from the Land to join Yosef and sons, thereby uniting a total of seventy family members in Egypt (cf. Ex. 1:1-5).

? *Read Genesis 10. Seventy sons are listed (14 from Yefet; 30 from Cham; 26 from Shem). These become the nations of the world [R' Bachya]. Explain the importance of uniting 70 sons and grandsons in exile as a nation-in-embryo.*

Family United

> ❝ Ya'akov sent Y'hudah ahead of him to Yosef, so that the latter might guide him on the road to Goshen; thus they arrived in the land of Goshen. ❞
> —Genesis 46:28-29a

Yosef himself harnesses his chariot to meet Yisra'el, his father, at Goshen (Gen. 46:29). The two embrace for a long time, in complete unity. Yisra'el tells Yosef, "Now I can die, because I have seen your face and seen that you are still alive" (Gen. 46:30).

The two names Ya'akov and Yisra'el are often used interchangeably. Ya'akov goes into exile from B'er Shava (Gen. 28:10; 46:1-5). Ya'akov sends ahead to the displaced firstborn (Gen. 32:3/4 הנ"ך; 46:28). But Yisra'el—not Ya'akov—acts as head of the future nation. Yisra'el alone is patriarch of his nation, b'nei Yisra'el, *the children of Yisra'el* (Gen. 46:30; 48:11, 14, 20). His presence helps unify the family.

Yisra'el unites the family by moving to Egypt.

In fact, vaYESHEV Yisra'el (*Israel dwells*) in Goshen, growing explosively from extended family into a young nation (Gen. 47:27). How ironic that Yisra'el enters nationhood in exile, outside the Land!

? Yisra'el's journey helps to unify a family into a nation. Read John 17:20-23. Note Yeshua's prayer for unborn generations, his seed-in-embryo. How can the Father's love for His Son help unify a family of nations into a kingdom?

Land

> " *Yosef found a place for his father and brothers and gave them property in the land of Egypt, in the best region of the country, in the land of Ra'amses, as Pharaoh had ordered.* "
> —Genesis 47:11

Yosef provides land near the town of Rameses in the area of Goshen—the best in Egypt!—to his father and brothers, according to Par'oh's command (Gen. 47:6, 11-12). Landholdings do not come easily (Gen. 17:8; 23:9, 20), but Yosef assigns the land as an achuzah (*permanent holding*).

> **Yosef provides his family with a permanent holding.**

The famine hits hard. Egyptians are forced to sell everything for food, including all their silver (Gen. 47:14), all their livestock (Gen. 47:17), and all their land (Gen. 47:19).

How ironic that the Egyptians lose everything. Finally, they are forced to sell themselves into bondage as slaves in order that they may "stay alive and not die" (Gen. 47:19; cf. Gen. 42:2; 43:8).

Yosef, once deprived of food and sold for silver by his brothers, only to be enslaved by Egyptians, now rations food, holds the silver, enslaves Egyptians, and saves his family from the effects of the famine.

> **?** *Read Ps. 126:4-6. Explain what Yosef sowed and reaped. Did the LORD wipe away every tear in Yosef's life? Read Rev. 21:4. In what ways can you walk in God's dreams for your life, watching Him wipe away tear after tear?*

Multiplying a Nation

> **❝** *Isra'el lived in the land of Egypt seventeen years. They acquired possessions in it and were productive, and their numbers multiplied greatly.* **❞**
> —Genesis 47:27

Multiplying into nationhood, the sons of Yisra'el are very fruitful, fulfilling promises made to Ya'akov (Gen. 28:3; 35:11). These promises are foundational to God's plan of redemption from the beginning of time (Gen. 1:28; 9:1, 7).

Yisra'el is blessed with prosperity and nationhood.

In Egypt, Yisra'el receives great blessing. Though others are forced to sell properties, the sons of Yisra'el actually acquire holdings (Gen. 47:27).

The population grows and spills into adjacent areas, establishing itself as a great nation in Egypt (Gen. 46:3).

Talmud comments that even as the people "acquire" land holdings, the land holdings "grasp" the people. Establishing security in land holdings can come at the cost of losing sojourner status, dependent solely on the promises of God [Stone, p. 267, n27 cites Ibn Ezra, Kli Yakar, and Midrash]. The nation risks "holding" on in Egypt for too long (Gen. 15:13).

> **?** Read Gen. 15:13-14. What is the result of grasping land holdings for too long? Explain why God would promise to bring us out of Egypt with great wealth, when the wealth tempts us to grasp security in place of God's word.

Meander

❝ *"The nations will know that I am ADONAI, who sets Isra'el apart as holy, when my sanctuary is with them forever."* **❞**

—*Ezekiel 37:28*

Reunion in Egypt highlights the activity of the Torah portion and forms the context for the Haftarah. In this reading, Y'hudah has matured into the nation that gives spiritual direction, but it has been exiled for seventy years from the Temple site. The tribes have matured, but they lead disconnected lives. Brotherly hatred has replaced brotherly love!

Now the prophet Y'chezkel (*Ezekiel*), in exile with his people, promises complete restoration between the tribes led by Y'hudah and the ten lost tribes led by Yosef's son Efrayim. Indeed, the two kingdoms will be united under a king from Y'hudah (Ez. 37:22, 24).

God promises to reconcile Yisra'el and Y'hudah and dwell among them.

The LORD promises to purify his people into a holy kingdom (Ez. 37:23). He promises a covenant of peace, and a Sanctuary in which He will dwell among His people. Only then will the nation find its place among the nations of the world.

? *Recall that in 721 B.C.E., the Assyrians led idolatrous Yisra'el into an exile without end. Yet a century and a half later, Ezekiel prophesies reunion! How can the ten lost tribes of Yosef be reunited with the kingdom of Y'hudah?*

...ings

❝ When day came, he called his talmidim and chose from among them twelve to be known as emissaries . . . and Y'hudah from K'riot, who turned traitor. ❞   —Luke 6:12, 16b

Yeshua, son of David, son of Y'hudah, begins to redeem the prophecy of Ezekiel. He comes when Rome is the world empire with Hordos (*Herod*), an

> **Yeshua selects twelve "sh'lichim" to unify Yisra'el into one nation.**

Edomite, in charge.

In this reading, Yeshua devotes all night to prayer for the purpose of selecting from his disciples twelve apostles as foundation stones (Lk. 6:13; Eph. 2:20). The Hebrew equivalent of apostle, shaliach,

describes *one who is sent forth* with the message and authority of the one who sent Him. Yeshua represents Himself as a shaliach of the LORD (Jn. 5:19, 24, 30, 37-38).

Here, Yeshua selects the twelve to represent corporate Yisra'el. It is curious that Y'hudah Ish-K'riot (*Judas Iscariot, the man from Kerioth*) comes from a town in the heartland of Y'hudah (Josh. 15:25). How ironic that Y'hudah's own nation must be purified of men who sin against the Father by selling a brother for silver. Y'hudah's drawing near and Yisra'el's coming out from

? *Read John 14:22. Notice that the other Y'hudah selected as shaliach asks why Yeshua will not reveal his identity (as viceroy to God's empire on earth). Explain why Yeshua keeps hidden his spiritual role as Mashiach ben Yosef.*

Oasis

Talk Your Walk . . .

Y'hudah draws near to the viceroy of Egypt to begin the longest speech recorded in Torah. His humility and leadership among the brothers is surpassed only by his love for his father. Faced with the agonized reality that the viceroy will imprison Binyamin, Y'hudah makes good on his pledge to his father to offer his own life for Binyamin's; and he does so in abject humility. Quoting Ya'akov, he explains that his father's favored wife bore him two sons. On one level, he diminishes his own sonship to clearly explain his father's urgent need to see Binyamin again. At the cost of his own life, and out of loving concern for his father, Y'hudah offers himself in Binyamin's stead—to safeguard his father from a new round of grief.

When brother reconciles with brother, the LORD grows a nation.

To his profound surprise, the viceroy of Egypt is Ya'akov's other "lost" son, Yosef. The brothers reconcile, and then the whole family can be healed! Par'oh hears about the meeting and commands wagons to be sent for Ya'akov. Later, Ya'akov gets the divine okay—in spite of his apprehension over another leave from the Promised Land. Once again, VAYISHLACH Ya'akov (*and Jacob sent*)—this time, he sends Y'hudah to scout Yosef in Egypt. Yosef will settle his father and family in the fertile land of Goshen. There, God destines His people to be fruitful, multiply, and grow into full-fledged nationhood.

. . . Walk Your Talk

Proverbs exhorts us to walk in wisdom, knowing that as a man sows, so shall he reap. Can you think of any times in your life when you have sown thorns in the lives of others—only to have the tables turned on you? Nowhere is this principle more clearly illustrated than in today's portion. VAYIGASH Y'hudah (*and Judah drew near*) in heroic, loving self-sacrifice to spare his father from heart-wrenching grief.

The LORD draws near to all nations by sending His son, Yeshua, to offer His life. Yeshua, a son of Y'hudah, will be sold for silver by yet another son of Y'hudah. His heroic act of self-sacrifice will redeem the nations in the same way that the korban pesach (*paschal lamb offering*) redeems Yisra'el out of Egypt.

Are you prepared to draw near? Are you willing to reconcile with all persons in your life—no matter what the personal cost? Will you offer your life solely to please the Father and bring rest to your soul? If so, then rejoice! You are willing to be completely sold out to God. Now

> *Drawing near brings the unity needed to save mankind.*

ask God to set the circumstances so you can walk your talk and seek His highest good in your life. Draw near to God, and He will draw near to you!

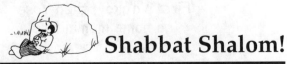

Shabbat Shalom!

וַיְחִי and Ya'akov lived on
through his sons.
Y'hudah and Yosef
weren't the only ones.
Adopting Efrayim and M'nasheh
—Egyptians—
he dreamed of a nation
with godly ambitions.

Ya'akov blessed Y'hudah
just before he died—
"The scepter of rulership
stays by his side.
Mashiach will come forth
from his tribe!"
First Ya'akov, then Yosef
go home mummified!

Walk VAY'CHI!
47:28-50:26

ויחי

And he lived

TORAH—Genesis 47:28-50:26
  1st Living in Eternal Promises—Genesis 47:28
  2nd Adopting a K'hilah—Genesis 48:10
  3rd Elevating the Second Born—Genesis 48:17
  4th Choosing the Ruler—Genesis 49:1
  5th Rewarding Unity—Genesis 49:19
  6th Blessing the Tribes—Genesis 49:27
  7th Comforted in Exile—Genesis 50:21
  Maftir Fullness of Years—Genesis 50:26

HAFTARAH—1 Kings 2:1-12
  Passing the Heritage—1 Kings 2:12

B'RIT CHADASHAH—1 Peter 1:1-9
  Inheriting the Blessing—1 Peter 1:9

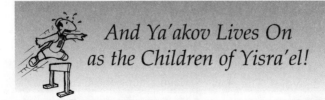

*And Ya'akov Lives On
as the Children of Yisra'el!*

Hiker's Log

← Looking Back

B'REISHEET (*in the beginning*), God commands man to be fruitful, multiply, fill the earth, and subdue it. Man disobeys, choosing a path that leads to destruction, exile, and death. Only **NOACH** (*Noah/rest*) finds chen (*favor*) and rests in God. In obedience, he builds an ark and becomes the only father to survive.

Ten generations of fathers live to witness Avram's birth; but Noach dies before Avram hears God call, **LECH L'CHA** (*go forth, yourself!*). Avraham immediately walks in God's word to him. Soon **VAYERA** YHWH (*and the LORD appeared*), to bring about Yitzchak's miraculous birth and salvation. The LORD swears the promised nation will be indestructible, ekev (*as a result/on the heel of*) Avraham's obedience to God's voice. The eternal promise of land and seed progresses through **CHAYEI SARAH** (*the life of Sarah*), with Rivkah as the next matriarch. **TOL'DOT** (*generations*) extend the land and seed inheritance of Avraham to Yitzchak's household and beyond.

> **B'REISHEET** *God creates.*
> *Only* **NOACH** *rests.*
> *God calls,* **LECH L'CHA.**
> **VAYERA**! *God announces Yitzchak.*
> **CHAYEI SARAH** *continues*
> *through* **TOL'DOT.**
> **VAYETSE, VAYISHLACH,**
> **VAYESHEV—**
> *Ya'akov exits, sends gifts,*
> *and resettles as Yosef* underscore{unsettles.}
> **MIKETZ**—*at the end,*
> *Y'hudah draws near*—**VAYIGASH!**
> *The family reunites,*
> **VAY'CHI**—*and Ya'akov lives on*
> *as the children of Yisra'el!*

VAYETSE Ya'akov (*and Jacob went out*) to escape Esav's wrath and avoid intermarriage among the C'na'anim.

Ya'akov comes back over twenty years later, vaYISHLACH (*and he sent*) tribute, returning to Esav the stolen blessing of pre-eminence. Then, having learnt the lessons of exile, vaYESHEV Ya'akov (*and Jacob settled*) in the Land. His family fragments, however—Y'hudah inter-married, Yosef in exile.

miKETZ (*at the end of*) years in jail, Yosef is ele-vated to viceroy of Egypt, where he forces his starv-ing brothers to face the hurts they inflicted long ago. Conflict among brothers must be redeemed. vaYIGASH Y'hudah (*and Judah drew near*), to stop the cycle of hurting the father. Ya'akov journeys to Egypt, and the family is unified at last! vaY'CHI Ya'akov (*and Jacob lived*) his last 17 years in Yosef's house-

In VAY'CHI . . .

The Key People include Ya'akov (*Jacob*), Yosef (*Joseph*), Efrayim (*Ephraim*), M'nasheh (*Manasseh*), all the sons, and Par'oh (*Pharaoh*).

The Scenes include Mitzrayim (*Egypt*), C'na'an (*Canaan*), Sh'chem (*Shechem*), cave of Machpelah, Goshen, and Avel Mitzrayim (*Abel-mizraim*).

The Main Events include Ya'akov's 17 years in Egypt, request for burial with fathers, adoption of Efrayim and M'nasheh, younger son getting the bigger blessing, Ya'akov's final words for each tribe, Y'hudah's position of praise, Ya'akov's death, burial in C'na'an, brothers fearing Yosef again, Yosef's reassurance, and Yosef's death at 110—declaring God will bring them out again and they must carry his bones back to rest in the Land.

hold. The stage is set for explosive growth, as the fami-ly matures into nationhood.

The Trail Ahead ➡

Compass Work

The Path

וַיְחִי יַעֲקֹב בְּאֶרֶץ מִצְרַיִם
שְׁבַע עֶשְׂרֵה שָׁנָה
וַיְהִי יְמֵי יַעֲקֹב שְׁנֵי חַיָּיו
שֶׁבַע שָׁנִים
וְאַרְבָּעִים וּמְאַת שָׁנָה

—בראשית מז/כח

letter:	yod	chet	yod	vav
	י	חֶ	יְ	וַ
sound:	EE	**CHee**	Y'	Vah

and he lived = VAY'CHI = וַיְחִי

The Legend

and lived Jacob	va-y'chi Ya'akov	וַיְחִי יַעֲקֹב
in the land of Egypt	b'erets Mitsrayim	בְּאֶרֶץ מִצְרַיִם
17 year(s)	sh'va esreh shanah	שְׁבַע עֶשְׂרֵה שָׁנָה
& it was days of Jacob	va-y'hi y'mei-Ya'akov	וַיְהִי יְמֵי־יַעֲקֹב
years of life-his	sh'nei chayav	שְׁנֵי חַיָּיו
7 years	sheva shanim	שֶׁבַע שָׁנִים
and 40	v'arba'im	וְאַרְבָּעִים
and 100 year(s)	oo-m'at shanah	וּמְאַת שָׁנָה׃

—*Genesis 47:28*

Related Words

living, alive	chai	חַי
fresh water, spring water (living water)	mayim chayim	מַיִם חַיִּים
I swear! Upon your life!	chayecha!	חַיֶּיךָ!
Cheers! To life!	l'chayim	לְחַיִּים
Book of Life	sefer ha-chayim	סֵפֶר הַחַיִּים
tree of life	ets chayim	עֵץ חַיִּים
long life, Methuselah's span	chayei M'tushelach	חַיֵּי מְתוּשֶׁלַח
eternal life	chayei olam, chayei ad	חַיֵּי עוֹלָם, חַיֵּי עַד

Hit the Trail!

Living in Eternal Promises

> ❝ *Ya'akov lived in the land of Egypt seventeen years; thus Ya'akov lived to be 147 years old.* ❞
> —Genesis 47:28

Locating the beginning of this portion in a Torah scroll is particularly challenging, because the usual spacing cues are missing. All other portions are delineated on the scroll by an empty space either nine letters wide or one complete line high. But here, no space marks the beginning of this new portion. Called a stumah (*closed section*), it is as if VAYIGASH (*drew near*) this portion. Such poetry in motion—one *draws near* in order to *live on!*

Ya'akov lives seventeen more years in Egypt, under the watch care of Yosef who closes his eyes. Recall that Yosef lived his first seventeen years as a lad in Ya'akov's house (Gen. 37:1-2a).

Ya'akov dies in Egypt, but dwells forever in the Land.

Before dying, Ya'akov asks Yosef to show him chen (*grace*) and swear that he will grant him chesed ve'emet (*kindness and truth*) by burying him with his fathers. Dutifully, the sons will carry him back, and Ya'akov shall dwell in the Land!

Read 1 Cor. 13:13. What three things remain forever? Ya'akov feared getting "grasped" by the land of Egypt.
• *Explain how Ya'akov's life continues as his sons carry out his hope to be buried with his fathers.*

Adopting a K'hilah

> **Now Isra'el's eyes were dim with age, so that he could not see. Yosef brought his sons near to him, and he kissed them and embraced them.**
>
> —Genesis 48:10

Half blind and nearing death, Yisra'el, like his father Yitzchak before him, gathers his sons to bless them. Placing Yosef's sons on his knees, Ya'akov adopts Efrayim and M'nasheh as his own (Gen. 48:5, 12). The adoption assures them equal portions in the Land [Sforno].

Ya'akov adopts sons as an assembly of peoples.

No ordinary adoption, Ya'akov recalls the promise God made at Beit-El (Gen. 35:9-13)—that Ya'akov would inherit a nation and also a kahal goyim (*congregation of nations*), and that he would live on the Land as an achuzat olam (*eternal possession*).

At the time, Ya'akov had eleven sons. He assumed wrongly after receiving the promise, that his wives would bear him additional sons for a community [Rashi from Pesikta in Stone, p. 270, n.4]. Instead, Ya'akov now looks upon Yosef (previously presumed dead), together with his sons, as "returned to life." In adopting Yosef's two sons by Os'nat the Egyptian, Ya'akov embraces the promise for a k'hilah—a kahal amim (*assembly of peoples*, see Gen. 48:4).

? Study Gen. 35:1-7, 10-11. Why did God give Ya'akov both a nation and a community of nations? Why must Ya'akov bury all the idols? How does El Beit-El (*God's House*) relate to Sh'lomo haMelech's Temple (1 Ki. 8:41-43)?

Elevating the Second-Born

> **"** When Yosef saw that his father was laying his right hand on Efrayim's head, it displeased him, and he lifted up his father's hand to . . . place it instead on M'nasheh's head. **"** —Genesis 48:17

Displeased about the reversal of his sons' birthright, Yosef attempts to manipulate his father's hand. But Ya'akov attempted nothing less at his father's deathbed (Gen. 27:19).

Efrayim is blessed as pre-eminent over the firstborn.

Yosef's line will inherit the rights of the firstborn (Gen. 48:5; 1 Chr. 5:1-2). Yosef wants, in turn, to reserve the best for his firstborn, M'nasheh. However, the seed of Efrayim (*fruitful*) is destined to fill the nations (Gen. 48:19). It is a "peculiar expression of populousness" [Dt. 33:17; Skinner, p. 50b] that connotes fruitfulness of land and seed.

Y'hoshua (*Joshua*), an Efrayimite, will lead the nation and apportion land to the tribes. M'nasheh camps under Efrayim's standard during the conquest (Num. 2:18-20), and the prince of Efrayim brings his offering before the prince of M'nasheh (Num. 7:48, 54). To expectations that Efrayim will be most numerous, census time comes twice; and his tribe ranks tenth, then eleventh!

> Read Gen. 17:4-6, 35:11. Efrayim is blessed with populousness. He jumps off to a promising start in obtaining the eternal land holdings to support growth. But the expected large numbers fail (Num. 1:32-33; 2:19). Explain.

Choosing the Ruler

> ❝ Then Ya'akov called for his sons and said, "Gather yourselves together, and I will tell you what will happen to you in the acharit-hayamim." ❞
>
> —Genesis 49:1

Ya'akov addresses every son as a tribal chief in the blessings said from his deathbed, reserved for the end of days. Prosperity and blessing are the central themes [Sailhamer, p. 277].

> *Ya'akov blesses his sons to prosper at the end of time.*

Starting with R'uven, the eldest and natural choice for firstborn blessing, Ya'akov eliminates each son until Y'hudah is declared heir to the blessing of pre-eminence. His brothers will bow down (cf. Gen. 37:10), and he will emerge as heir to the throne (Gen. 49:10; Ps. 78:68, 70).

Though not the start of the r'vi'i (*fourth*) reading, Y'hudah's blessing (Gen. 49:8) is distinctive; it always heads a new column on the Torah scroll! Y'hudah heads all tribes, even Yosef (Ps. 78:67-68, 2:6-8; Dan. 7:13-14; Rev. 5:5, 9). What begins centuries later with King David (2 Sam 5:2-3) will climax in a dynasty of kings. Early rabbinic sources had no problem seeing Messiah at the end of this kingly line [Targ. Onkelos, Sanh. 98b, Zohar 1:25b].

> **?** Read Gen. 49:1-28. Are there any sons who are not blessed with prosperity or invincibility? If Yosef has the right of firstborn, explain why pre-eminence over his brothers is not his right, too (Gen. 49:8; cf. 1 Chr. 5:1-2).

Rewarding Unity

❝ *"Gad [troop]—a troop will troop on him, but he will troop on their heel."* ❞

—Genesis 49:19

Mysterious beginning for a segment to start with Gad! The previous verse delineates the blessing for Dan, Rachel's concubine's firstborn son.

Here, the blessing is reserved for Leah's concubine's firstborn. Gad will have success at maintaining secure borders against wandering nomads on the fringe.

> **Gad will hold his land against marauders.**

Historically, Gad supported unity by crossing the Yarden (*Jordan*) to help his brothers conquer lands with Y'hoshua on the west side (Josh. 4:12; 22:1-4), thus fulfilling a promise to Moshe (Num. 32:17-22, 27, 32).

Gad's assimilation by the Assyrian Tiglath Pileser III renders the idea of invincibility questionable, despite former glories against the Hagrites (1 Chr. 5:18-22).

Gad's destiny is tied to Yisra'el, a nation that supported idolatrous kings. But Yisra'el scorned the covenant and lost a prosperous life in the Land.

? The longest blessings are reserved for Y'hudah (Gen. 49:8-12) and Yosef (Gen. 49:22-26). But the segments split blessings reserved for the firstborns of the concubines. Explain why so much attention is given to the firstborns.

Blessing the Tribes

> ❝ *"Binyamin is a ravenous wolf, in the morning devouring the prey, in the evening still dividing the spoil."* ❞
>
> —Genesis 49:27

The youngest son, Binyamin, is last to be blessed. As the father's pampered child, Binyamin, the son, is anything but the wolf which describes the tribal blessing.

> **The last son is blessed as a fiercely successful warrior.**

Binyamin will mature into this wolf, as the tribe matures in its blessing. This will become evident in Ehud's battle with Moav (Jd. 3:15-30); in its skilled battle, when outnumbered, against a united Yisra'el (Jd. 20:12-25); and ultimately in the selection (1 Sam. 9:1-2) of the first king of Yisra'el—King Sha'ul (*Saul*).

The beginning of this segment puzzles me, since so many of the segments and portion names give forward movement to the story line (of God's work to redeem, prosper, and return man to Gan Eden as co-creator and co-partner of an on-going work). It is surprising that Ya'akov's death and burial are included in this segment, headed by a one-verse blessing of Binyamin.

> *Read Gen. 49:3-4, 5-7, 14-15, 13, 20. Most sons receive blessing from Ya'akov. Even where blame is heavy (e.g. Levi), note how the priestly blessing for Levi unfolds. Explain why Binyamin is highlighted for the final blessing.*

Comforted in Exile

> ❝ "... So don't be afraid—I will provide for you and your little ones." In this way, he comforted them, speaking kindly to them. ❞
>
> —Genesis 50:21

Compassion prevails! The brothers have renewed fears after the passing of their father. Remember that Esav planned to kill his brother after his father's death (Gen. 27:41).

Yosef comforts his brothers after their father's death.

Yosef speaks words of comfort and reassurance to his brothers. Even as Lemech looked upon his son, Noach, and said y'nachamenu (*he will comfort us*) in Gen. 5:29, vay'nachem Yosef (*and Joseph comforts*) and speaks to the heart of his brothers, pledging anew to preserve the sons of Yisra'el and their families (Gen. 50:21).

With these words, Yosef walks in the mantle of Noach, patriarch of the firstborns. As Noach's birth signalled the easing of the curse on the ground, now Yosef's provision of Goshen grants fertile ground and safety for the newly developing nation-in-embryo destined to reach the world with the saving faith of Avraham.

? Redemption does not tarry—it waits for man to make right choices in walking with God. Explain how Yosef continues the progress of mankind in fulfilling God's command to be fruitful, multiply, fill the earth, and subdue it.

Fullness of Years

> **" So Yosef died at the age of 110, and they embalmed him and put him in a coffin in Egypt. "**
> —*Genesis 50:26*

Yosef lives the ideal Egyptian life span of 110 years. The crowning joy of a full life is to see one's grandchildren [Ps. 128:6; Prov. 17:6; Is. 53:10, cited in Hamilton, p. 710].

> *Yosef lives a full life and dreams beyond.*

Yosef lives to see sons of his grandson, Machir (Gen. 50:23). Machir (*one who is sold*) has an identification with Yosef that goes beyond adoption. His great grandchildren will include the daughters of Tselof'chad, who inherit the Land (Num. 36:10-12).

Yosef dies and is placed in an aron (*ark*). Yet his hopes live on. He presses his brothers to swear to bury him in the Land. Much later, when the sons of Yisra'el are redeemed, Yosef travels the wilderness in one aron, and the tablets of the Decalogue travel in a second aron (Dt. 10:5).

Commenting, the author of the book of Hebrews punctuates Yosef's hopes and directions concerning burial as actions of a hero of the faith (Heb. 11:22; Gen. 50:24-25).

> **?** Recall that Avraham lived 175 = 7 x 5x5
> Yitzchak lived 180 = 5 x 6x6
> Ya'akov lived 147 = 3 x 7x7
> Explain this: Yosef lives 110 = 1 x 5x5 + 6x6 + 7x7

Meander

Dynasty begins as kingly rule passes from father to son. David lives on through Sh'lomo (*Solomon*) his son, and David's house lives on through the reign of Sh'lomo haMelech (*King Solomon*).

David haMelech passes a heritage to his son.

Both David and Sh'lomo reign for a full 40-year generation. Thus, the dynasty of the line of Y'hudah begins auspiciously with a passing of the heritage from father to son.

To ensure Sh'lomo's firm control, David instructs his son to beware his enemies. Yoav and Shimei must be dealt with (2 Sam. 3:27; 1 Ki. 2:5-6, 8-9) in order to secure lasting control.

The dynasty continues! Matthew's genealogy telescopes the generations into chunks of fourteen (the numerical sum of the Hebrew letters in David's name)—from Avraham to David, to Y'chanyah (*Jeconiah*, also called *Coniah*) in the Babylonian exile, and another fourteen generations to Yeshua, son of Yosef by adoption.

? *Read Mt. 1:17. Explain why the Babylonian exile has meaning in the context of a dynasty passing across the generations from father to son, starting with David and Sh'lomo. How can David's hopes live on in Yeshua?*

...ings

** And you are receiving what your trust is aiming at, namely, your deliverance. **

—1 Peter 1:9

Salvation of our souls is the goal of our faith! The outcome of this goal will be revealed at the last day. Meanwhile, how does one prepare?

Heirs inherit the blessings by waiting faithfully.

In Yisra'el's case, the eternal land and seed heritage blessings must be appropriated in faith, with the saving of the nation as the ultimate outcome of faith (Ro. 11:25-27).

For Yisra'el and believers alike, our inheritance is reserved; and believers are protected until they come into the inheritance by God's power. Until then, one waits with joy to inherit the blessing (1 Pet. 1:8).

Even life's valuables, such as fine gold, are perishable (1 Pet. 1:18). But faith, like the inheritance for which it waits, is indestructible and eternal [Michaels, p.30]. Faith is perfected through life's trials (1 Pet. 1:6b-7); and it evokes praise, honor, and glory in the day God appears for the saving of souls.

? Read 1 Peter 1:6b-7. Fullness of faith comes as a result of surviving life's tests and trials. The process can be compared to the purifying of gold in a smelter. How can you stand the heat? Explain how one renews under pressure.

Oasis

Talk Your Walk . . .

Ya'akov moves to Egypt, with God's assurance that Yosef will close his eyes. A symmetry of experience occurs—Yosef, raised in Ya'akov's house for 17 years, now provides for his father for 17 years. Father and son have switched positions. Yosef will show chen (*grace*) to his father and swear to bury him with his fathers, at Machpelah.

Before Ya'akov dies, Yosef brings his two sons to their half-blind grandfather for adoption. Ya'akov claims these two as his own sons, implicitly bestowing upon Yosef a double portion in the Land. Ya'akov crosses his hands to bless the younger one, Efrayim, as pre-eminent. He insists that Efrayim (*fruitful*) will become a kahal amim (*community of peoples*). The blessing opens the door for the adoption of gentile nations in the days following Messiah's death.

On his deathbed, Ya'akov calls in all his sons for the final blessing. Suspense unfolds as the first three sons are eliminated from the firstborn's blessing. Y'hudah, however, emerges as leader and heir to the promise of a dynasty of kings. Others receive blessings of military prowess. Then Ya'akov dies. His sons carry him back to the Land. Upon return, Yosef addresses his brothers' fears, reassuring them that what they meant for evil God has used for good. Yosef dies at 110 and awaits the exodus and burial in the Land of Promise.

> *And Ya'akov lives on as the children of Israel.*

. . . Walk Your Talk

Is there life after death? The kings promised to Avraham, to rule over the Land of Promise, do not begin to rule until King David comes, more than eight hundred years later. Yet King David, who begins this dynasty of kings in Y'rushalayim, is assured by God that he will always have an ancestor, born of his loins, to dwell upon the throne. Surely David wonders what will become of him, before he concludes: You will not abandon my soul to Sh'ol (Ps. 16:10). The path of life, fullness of joy, and everlasting bliss come from being seated at the right hand of God!

For the righteous, fellowship with God remains unbroken through death. Herein lies the starting point for the reign of eternal life in our time-bound world.

Are you living in an everlasting covenant relationship with God? Is your relationship with God an eternal one? Do your actions reflect your deepest hopes to abide forever in the Presence of God? Ya'akov lives forever, as

> *Unbroken fellowship begins when Yeshua abides in your soul.*

Yisra'el, the father of his people. His genes, his memory, and his body still dwell in the Land along with his people. Has God forsaken his soul to lay in the dust? How can you choose to inherit along with him?

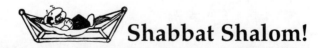 **Shabbat Shalom!**

Journey's End

In one sense, humankind dies without being able to see the hope of redemption. God is with us, but we cannot see Him. Yeshua lives as Imanu-El (*God with us*), but we do not have the eyes to see.

Even the heroes of the faith who "walked with" God have not seen clearly from afar. Adam did not live to see Chanoch taken. Chanoch did not live to see Noach survive the flood. Noach did not live to see the calling of Avraham. Avraham did not live to see Ya'akov become Yisra'el.

The blessing and direction have always been the same.

All these saw and understood from afar, with only partial understanding.

Nevertheless, these same heroes of the faith still "walked with" God on the eternal path of redemption, and they experienced the everlasting Presence of God. Chanoch escaped death. Noach survived the flood and lived to see the tenth generational son. Avraham inherited God's covenant, heard God swear he would father an everlasting nation, and saw the covenant become the heritage of his only son and his grandson, too. Finally, Yisra'el watched his family of tribal chieftains reconcile. Now unified and safely transplanted to the incubator in Egypt, Yisra'el's nation-in-embryo entered explosive growth.

The blessing has always been the same—be fruitful, multiply, fill the earth, and subdue it! The direction has always been the same, too—walk with God and live eternally in His Presence!!

Are you committed to walking with your Father Who is in heaven? Are you indwelt by Imanu-El (*God with us*)? Has Messiah redeemed you from the selfish path that leads to cursing, exile, destruction, and death? Do you experience the abiding Presence of God in your life?

The scriptures teach, "You have been born again not from some seed that will decay, but from one that cannot decay, through the living Word of God that lasts forever" (1 Peter 1 :23). God's Word not only abides in us, but takes on a life of its own within us!

Renew your commitment to study the Word, and let its life flow within your heart. Then the words you speak will return to you as a pathway to redemption. Do you believe God can guide you? Are you ready to walk in the highest dreams God has for your life? God made Avraham the "Father of Many Nations," because he listened to God's voice and acted on his heels to follow God's instruction. Are you ready to jump in obedience??

Strengthen yourself in God's Word. Journey on through the scriptures. Study, meditate, and reflect on the Word.

> ### *Let us live in God's Word and be strengthened!*

Abide in the Presence of God, and, in humility, let scripture and prayer inform the decisions of your life. Chazak, chazak, v'nitchazek (*Be strong, be strong, and may we be strengthened*)!!!

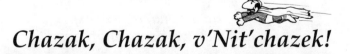

Chazak, Chazak, v'Nit'chazek!

חֲזַק חֲזַק

וְנִתְחַזֵּק!!!

Well, that's the end
of the Genesis story.
You can rest on your journey
and worship God's glory!
Then the beat goes on—
let the Torah roll
Through Exodus, Leviticus,
and the rest of the scroll.
At the end of each book,
we take a break.
Chazak, Chazak, v'Nit'chazek!

חזק חזק ונתחזק
*Be strong, be strong,
and may we be strengthened!!!*

Glossary

Ach'**av** (*Ahab*)

achi**chem** (*your brother*)

achu**zah** (*permanent holding*)

A**dam** (*Adam/humankind*)

a**dam** (*man, mankind*)

ada**mah** (*ground*)

ADONAI (*The LORD/YHWH*)

ADONAI nit**sav** a**lav** (*the LORD was standing upon him/it*)

ado**ni** (*my lord*)

Adoni**yahu** (*Adonijah*)

ake**dah** (*binding*)

ali**yah** (*immigration*)

Ami**dah** (benedictions prayed while *standing*)

'Amo**rah** (*Gomorrah*)

Ani Yo**sef!** (*I am Yosef!*)

ano**chi** e**red** im**cha** (*I will go down with you*), v'ano**chi** a'al**cha** gam a'**lot** (*and I will also bring you back up*)

a**ron** (*ark*)

Arpach**shad** (*Arphaxad*)

a**sham** (*guilt offering*)

av (*father*)

A**vel** Mitzra**yim** (*Abel-mizraim*)

Avi**melech** (*Abimelech*)

Avra**ham** (*Abraham/father of a multitude of nations*)

A**vram** (*Abram/exalted father*)

'**Azza** (*Gaza*)

ba**lal** (*confusion*)

Bat-**Shua** (*daughter of Shua*)

Bat-**Sheva** (*Bathsheba*)

ba**vel** (*Babel, babble*)

Beit-**El** (*Bethel*)

ben (*son*)

B'**er Sha**va (*Beersheba, the well of swearing*)

Binya**min** (*Benjamin*)

b'**nei** a**dam** (*sons of Adam/mankind*)

B'REISHEET (*in the beginning*)

B'**rit** Chada**shah** (*New Covenant*/New Testament)

b'**rit** o**lam** (*everlasting covenant*)

b'ya**dam** (*in their hands*)

Cham (*Ham*)

chamas (*lawlessness*)

chamishi (*fifth*)

Chamor (*Hamor*)

Chanoch (*Enoch/disciple*)

Charan (*Haran/crossroads*)

Chavah (*Eve/mother of the living*)

CHAYEI SARAH (*the life of Sarah*)

Chazak, chazak, v'nitchazek (*Be strong, be strong, and may we be strengthened*)!!!

chen (*grace/favor*)

chesed ve'emet (*covenant loyalty and truthfulness*)

Chet (*Heth*)

Chevron (*Hebron*)

Chidekel (*Tigris*)

C'na'an (*Canaan*)

C'na'ani (*Canaanite*)

C'na'anim (*Canaanites*)

David haMelech (*King David*)

darga-t'vir (*rising and falling chanting marks*)

dod (*lover*)

Dotan (*Dothan*)

D'vorah (*Deborah*)

'ednah (*delicate skin, moist*)

Efrat (*Ephrath*)

Efrayim (*Ephraim/fruitful*)

Efron ben-Tsochar (*Ephron son of Zohar*)

ekev (*as a result/heel*)

ekev asher shamata b'koli (*as a result of your heel-like obedi-ence to my voice*)

El'chah! (*I will go! Gen. 45:28*)

Elech! (*I will go! Gen. 24:58*)

erebu (*Assyrian legal category*)

Esav (*Esau*)

Ever (*Eber/other side, across, see also Ivri*)

et-banav v'et-nasav (*his sons and his wives*)

et-nasav v'et-banav (*his wives and his sons*)

F'rat (*Euphrates*)

Gal'ed (*Galeed*)

Gan Eden (*the Garden of Eden*/Paradise)

Gat-Sh'manim (*Gethsemane*)

gematria (*calculation of numerical value of Hebrew words to search for hidden meanings; note Rev. 13:18*)

Gichon (*Gihon*)

G'rar (*Gerar*)

G'shu-na elai. (*Come close now, to me, please!*)

HA'AZINU (*give ear*)

Haftarah (*conclusion/ Prophets and Writings*)

Halachah (*Hebrew Law*)

haY'or (*the Nile*)

Hevel (*Abel, transitory* in Eccl.)

Hordos (*Herod*)

Imanu-El (*God with us*)

ish (*man*)

Ivri (*Hebrew*/one who *crosses over*)

Ivrim (*Hebrews*)

Izevel (*Jezebel*)

Kach-na et birchati (*take please my gifts/my blessing*)

kaddish (*sanctification*)

kahal/k'hilah (*congregation, assembly*)

kahal amim (*assembly or congregation of peoples*)

kahal goyim (*congregation of nations*)

Kayin (*Cain*)

Keinan (*Kenan*)

Kiryat Arba (*Kiriath-arba, now Hebron*)

ki-tov (*that it is good*)

kohanim (*priests*)

kol (*all*)

kol ha'aretz (*all the earth*)

korban pesach (*Passover Lamb/paschal lamb offering*)

Koresh (*Cyrus*)

k'ruvim (*cherubim/angels*)

K'turah (*Keturah*)

Lavan (*Laban*)

LECH L'CHA (*go forth, yourself!*)

Lemech (*Lamech*)

Machalat (*Mahalath*)

Machanayim (*Mahanaim/Twin Camps*)

machaneh (*camp*)

Machir (*Makir/one who is sold*)

maftir (*concluding*)

Mahalal'el (*Mahalalel*)

mal'achim (*messengers*)

Mashiach (*Messiah*)

Mashiach ben Yosef (*Messiah, son of Joseph*)

m'chiyah (*life saver*)

Melchi-Tsedek (*Melchizedek, lit. King of Righteousness*)

Midrash (*exposition, rabbinical commentary on the Bible*)

Midyan (*Midian*)

Midyanim (*Midianites*)

MIKETZ (*at the end of*)

mikveh (*gathering of, ritual bath, pool*)

minchah (*tribute*)

minyan (lit. *number/quorum of 10 adults for public prayer*)

Miryam (*Miriam*)

Mishkan (*Tabernacle/God's Dwelling*)

Mishnah (*teachings, the Oral Law compiled in 220 CE*)

Mitzrayim (*Egypt*)

M'nasheh (*Manasseh*)

Moav (*Moab*)

mohar (*bridal dowry*)

M'tushelach (*Methuselah*)

Nachor (*Nahor*)

Natan (*Nathan*)

N'tan'el (*Nathanael, Nathaniel*)

NOACH (*Noah/rest*)

Noachide (*having to do with Noah, also Noachic*)

Nod, an area east of Eden (*wandering or exile*)

N'vayot (*Nebaioth*)

olah (*ascent offering; burnt or whole offering*)

onen (*mourner*)

Os'nat (*Asenath*)

Ovadyahu (*Obadiah*)

parashah (Torah *portion*)

parashiot (Torah *portions*)

Par'oh (*Pharaoh*)

Peretz (*Perez*)

P'lishtim (*Philistines*)

P'ni'el (*Peniel*)

Potifar (*Potiphar*)

Rachav (*Rahab*)

Rav (*Rabbi/Great One*)

Rav 'od Yosef b'ni chai! El'chah. (*Great! Still Joseph my son lives!! I shall go.*)

R'chovot (*Rehoboth*)

rishon (*first*)

Rivkah (*Rebecca*)

R'u (*Reu*)

Ruach Elohim bo (*the Spirit of God in him, Gen. 41:38*)

Ruach haKodesh (*Holy Spirit*)

Rut (*Ruth*)

R'uven (*Reuben*)

r'vi'i (*fourth*)

sabbatismos (Greek for *rest*)

S'dom (*Sodom*)

Se'ir (*Seir*)

Shabbat (*Sabbath*)

Shalem (*Salem*)

shaliach (*apostle/one who is sent forth*)

Sha'ul (*Saul*)

Sh'chem (*Shechem*)

Shelach (*Shelah*)

shem (*name*)

sheni (*second*)

shesh (*fine linen*)

Shet (*Seth/appointed*)

Shim'on (*Simeon*)

Shin'ar (*Shinar*)

shishi (*sixth*)

shivah (*seven-day mourning period*)

Shiv'ah (*Shibah/seven*)

sh'lichim (*apostles*, pl. of shaliach)

shlishi (*third*)

Sh'lomo (*Solomon*)

Sh'lomo haMelech (*King Solomon*)

sh'ma (*hear, listen and obey*)

Sh'mot (*names/Exodus*)

Sh'ol (*abode of the dead*)

shvi'i (*seventh*)

Simchat Torah (*joy of the Torah*)

S'rug (*Serug*)

stumah (*closed section*)

Sukkot (*Succoth*)

Talmud (*commentary on the Mishnah*)

Terach (*Terah*)

t'hom (*the deep*)

Tol'dot (*generations, life story, offspring*)

Torah (*instruction*/Pentateuch, Gen.-Dt.)

tsadik (*righteous one*)

Tsaf'**nat**-Pa'neach (*Zaphenath Paneah, Yosef's new name*)

Tse'! (*Go out!*)

t'shu**vah** (*repentance*)

Tsi**lah** (*Zillah*)

Tsi**yon** (*Zion*)

Tso'ar (*Zoar*)

tsu**ris** (*grief; Yiddish term*)

Tuval-**Ka**yin (*Tubal-cain*)

Ur Cas**dim** (*Ur of the Chaldeans*)

vaya**kom** (*and he rose up*)

vaY'chi (*and he lived*)

vaYera (*and He appeared*)

vaYeshev (*and he settled*)

vaYetse (*and he went out*)

vaYigash (*and he drew near*)

vaYikra (*and He called/ Leviticus*)

vaYishlach (*and he sent*)

vay'na**chem** (*and he comforts*)

Ya'a**kov** (*Jacob/Heel-grabber/ Supplanter*)

Ya**bok** (*the Jabbok*)

Yarav'**am** (*Jeroboam*)

Yarden (*Jordan*)

Ya**val** (*Jabal*)

Y'chan**yah** (*Jeconiah*)

Y'chez**kel** (*Ezekiel*)

ye'a**vek** (*wrestles*)

Yefet (*Japheth*)

Yered (*Jared*)

Yeshua (*Jesus/salvation*)

Yeshua Bar **Ab**ba (*Barabbas/ lit. Jesus, Son of the Father*)

Yeshua haMashiach (*Jesus the Messiah*)

yeshu**ah** (*salvation*)

Y'ho**ram** (*Jehoram*)

Y'hoshua (*Joshua*)

Y'hu**dah** (*Judah*)

Y'hu**dah** Ish-K'ri**ot** (*Judas Iscariot/the man from Kerioth*)

Yishma'**el** (*Ishmael*)

Yishma'**elim** (*Ishmaelites*)

Yisra'**el** (*Israel*)

Yit**zchak** (*Isaac/laughter*)

y'nacha**me**nu (*he will comfort us*)

Yoav (*Joab*)

Yo**sef** (*Joseph*)

Y'rushala**yim** (*Jerusalem*)

Zerach (*Zerah*)

Bibliography

Alter, Robert. *The Art of Biblical Narrative*. Berkeley, CA: Basic Books, 1981.

Alter, Robert. *Genesis: Translation and Commentary*. First edition. New York: W. W. Norton & Company, 1996.

Attridge, Harold W. *The Epistle to the Hebrews*. In Helmut Koester (Gen. Ed.), *Hermeneia*. Philadelphia: Fortress Press, 1989.

Averbeck, Richard E. "Mikdash," in W. A.VanGemeren (Gen. Ed.), *New International Dictionary of Old Testament Theology and Exegesis* (Vol. 2, pp. 1078-1087). Grand Rapids, MI: Zondervan Publishing House, 1997.

Ben Avraham, Rabbi Alexander, and Sharfman, Rabbi Benjamin (Eds.). *The Pentateuch and Rashi's Commentary*. Brooklyn, NY: S. S. & R. Publishing Company, Inc. (also Philadelphia: Press of the Jewish Publication Society), 1976.

Bruce, F. F. *The New International Commentary on the New Testament: The Epistle to the Hebrews*. Grand Rapids, MI: Wm. B. Eerdmans Publishing Company, 1979.

Bullinger, E. W. *Figures of Speech Used in the Bible*. Grand Rapids, MI: Baker Book House, 1987. (Original work published in 1898).

Childs, Brevard S. *Biblical Theology of the Old and New Testaments: Theological Reflection on the Christian Bible*. Minneapolis: Fortress Press, 1993.

Cohen, A. (Gen. Ed.). *Soncino Books of the Bible*. Volumes 1-14. London: The Soncino Press Limited, 1978.

Concordance to the Novum Testamentum Graece. Third edition. Berlin: Walter De Gruyter, 1987.

Driver, S. R., Plummer, A., and Briggs, C. A. (Gen. Eds.). *The International Critical Commentary on the Holy Scriptures of the Old and New Testaments*. Edinburgh: T. & T. Clark, 1979. (Original work published 1896-1924).

Ellingworth, Paul. *The New International Greek New Testament Commentary: The Epistle to the Hebrews*. Grand Rapids, MI: William B. Eerdmans Publishing Company, 1993.

Elwell, W. A. (Ed.). *Evangelical Dictionary of Theology*. Grand Rapids, MI: Baker Book House, 1984.

Evans, Louis H., Jr. *The Communicator's Commentary: Hebrews*. Dallas: Word Publishing, 1985.

Even-Shoshan, Avraham (Ed.). *New Concordance for the Torah, Prophets, and Writings*. Jerusalem: Sivan Press, 1977.

Fox, Everett. *The Schocken Bible: The Five Books of Moses*. Volume I. Dallas: Word Publishing, 1995.

Family Chumash, see Scherman, Rabbi Nosson, et al.

Frankel, Ellen and Teutsch, Betsy P. (1992). *The Encyclopedia of Jewish Symbols*. Northvale, NJ: Jason Aronson, 1992.

Friedman, Rabbi Alexander Zusia. *Wellsprings of Torah*. Transl. by Gertrude Hirschler. New York: Judaica Press, Inc., 1990.

Gordon, Cyrus H. *Before the Bible*. New York: Harper and Row, 1962.

Hamilton, Victor P. *The New International Commentary on the Old Testament: The Book of Genesis*. Grand Rapids, MI: William B. Eerdmans Publishing Company, 1990.

Herczeg, Rabbi Yisrael Isser Zvi (Ed.). *The Torah: With Rashi's Commentary Translated, Annotated, and Elucidated*. Artscroll Series/The Sapirstein Edition. Brooklyn: Mesorah Publications, Ltd., 1995.

Hertz, Dr. J. H. (Ed.). *The Pentateuch and Haftorahs*. Second edition. London: Soncino Press, 1975.

Hirsch, Samson Raphael, Trans. *The Pentateuch, Haftarah, and the Five Megillot*. Ed. by Ephraim Oratz. New York: The Judaica Press, Inc., 1990. (English translation by Gertrude Hirschler; German work published in 1867-1878).

Holy Bible, New Living Translation. Wheaton, IL: Tyndale House Publishers, Inc., 1996. (Genesis translated by A. Ross, J. Sailhamer, and G. Wenham).

ibn Paquda, R. Bachya. *Duties of the Heart*. Transl. by Moses Hyamson. Jerusalem: Feldheim Publishers, 1986. (Translated from Arabic into Hebrew by R. Yehuda Ibn Tibbon).

Kahan, Rabbi Aharon. *The Taryag Mitzvos*. Brooklyn: Keser Torah Publications, 1988. (Based on the classical Sefer haChinuch).

Kantor, Mattis. *The Jewish Time Line Encyclopedia: A Year-by-Year History from Creation to the Present*. Northvale, NJ: Jason Aronson, Inc., 1989.

Keil, C. F. and Delitzsch, F. *Commentary on the Old Testament.*, Transl. by James Martin. Volumes 1-10. Grand Rapids, MI: William B. Eerdmans Publishing Company, 1976.

Kent, Homer A. *The Epistle to the Hebrews*. Grand Rapids, MI: Baker Book House, 1985.

Kohlenberger, John R. III (Ed.). *The NIV Interlinear Hebrew-English Old Testament*. Grand Rapids, MI: Zondervan Publishing House, 1979.

Kolatch, Alfred J. *The Complete Dictionary of English and Hebrew First Names*. Middle Village, NY: Jonathan David Publishers, Inc., 1984.

Lachs, Samuel Tobias. *A Rabbinic Commentary on the New Testament*. Hoboken, NJ: Ktav Publishing House, Inc., 1987.

Lane, William L. *Hebrews: A Call to Commitment*. Peabody, MA: Hendrickson Publishers, 1988.

Lane, William L. *Word Biblical Commentary: Hebrews 1-13*. Volumes 47a, 47b. Waco, TX: Word Books, Publisher, 1991.

Leibowitz, Nehama. *Studies in Bereshit (Genesis)*. Transl. by Aryeh Newman. Fourth revised edition. Jerusalem: Hemed Press, 1994.

Michaels, J. Ramsey. *Word Biblical Commentary: 1 Peter*. Volume 49. Waco, TX: Word Books, Publisher, 1988.

Nachshoni, Yehuda. *Studies in the Weekly Parashah*. Transl. by Shmuel Himelstein. Volume 1. Brooklyn: Mesorah Publications, Ltd., 1989.

The New English Bible. Standard edition. New York: Oxford
  University Press, 1971.
Novum Testamentum Graece. Nestle-Aland Edition. Stuttgart:
  Deutsche Bibelstiftung, 1981.
Plaut, W. Gunther. *The Haftarah Commentary.* Transl. by Chaim
  Stern. New York: UAHC Press, 1996.
Rashi, see Ben Avraham, Rabbi Abraham et al. or Herczek,
  Rabbi Yisrael Isser Zvi.
Robertson, A. T. *Word Pictures in the New Testament.* Grand
  Rapids, MI: Baker Book House, 1932.
Sailhamer, John H. *The Expositor's Bible Commentary: Genesis.*
  Volume 2. Grand Rapids, MI: Zondervan Publishing House,
  1990.
Sailhamer, John H. (1992). *The Pentateuch as Narrative.* Grand
  Rapids, MI: Zondervan Publishing House, 1992.
Scherman, Rabbi Nosson, and Zlotowitz, Rabbi Meir (Gen.
  Eds.). *The Family Chumash: Breishis.* Transl. by Rabbi Meir
  Zlotowitz. First edition. Brooklyn: Mesorah Publications, Ltd.,
  1989.
Scherman, Rabbi Nosson (Gen. Ed.). *The Chumash.* Ed. by
  Rabbi Hersh Goldwurn, Rabbi Avie Gold, and Rabbi Meir
  Zlotowitz. Artscroll Series, The Stone Edition. Brooklyn:
  Mesorah Publications, Ltd., 1995.
Schorr, Rabbi Yisroel Simcha (Gen. Ed.). *Talmud Bavli.* The
  Artscroll Series, Schottenstein Edition. Brooklyn: Mesorah
  Publications, Ltd., 1993.
Sforno, Ovadiah. *Commentary on the Torah.* Transl. by Rabbi
  Raphael Pelcovitz. The Artscroll Mesorah Series. Brooklyn:
  Mesorah Publications, Ltd., 1997.
Shulman, Eliezer. *The Sequence of Events in the Old Testament.*
  Transl. by Sarah Lederhendler. Fifth edition. Jerusalem:
  Investment Co. of Bank Hapoalim and Ministry of Defense—
  Publishing House, 1987.
Skinner, John. *The International Critical Commentary: Genesis.*
  Second edition. Edinburgh: T & T. Clark Ltd., 1994.

Speiser, E.A. *The Anchor Bible: Genesis, A New Translation with Introduction and Commentary.* New York: Doubleday, 1962.

Stern, David H., Trans. *Jewish New Testament.* Clarksville, MD: Jewish New Testament Publications, 1991.

Stern, David H. *Jewish New Testament Commentary.* Clarksville, MD: Jewish New Testament Publications, 1992.

Sternberg, Meir. *The Poetics of Biblical Narrative.* Bloomington: Indiana University Press, 1987.

Stone Edition, see Scherman, Rabbi Nosson (Gen. Ed.).

Tenney, Merrill C. *The Expositor's Bible Commentary: John.* Volume 9. Grand Rapids, MI: Zondervan Publishing House, 1981.

Tikkun Kor'im haM'fuar. Brooklyn, NY: Im haSefer, 1994.

Von Rad, Gerhard. *The Old Testament Library: Genesis.* Revised edition. Philadelphia: The Westminster Press, 1972.

Wenham, Gordon. *Word Biblical Commentary: Genesis.* Volumes 1-2. Dallas: Word Books, 1994.

Werblowsky, Dr. R. J. Zwi and Wigoder, Dr. Geoffrey (Eds.). *The Encyclopedia of the Jewish Religion.* Jerusalem: Masada Press Ltd., 1967.

Westermann, Claus. *Genesis, 1-50: A Commentary.* Transl. by J. J. Scullion. Minneapolis: Augsburg Publishing House, 1986.

Wigram, George V. *The Englishman's Hebrew and Chaldee Concordance of the Old Testament.* Grand Rapids, MI: Baker Book House, 1980. (Original work published in 1843).

Zornberg, Avivah Gottlieb. *Genesis: The Beginning of Desire.* Philadelphia: The Jewish Publication Society, 1995.